America, the Beautiful
Patriotic Activity Book

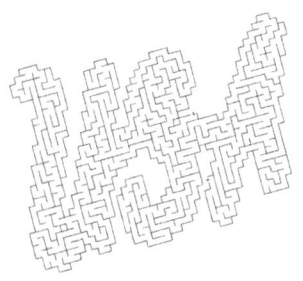

Featuring:
Coloring Pages
Color By Numbers
Cryptograms
Dot-to-Dot
Journal Pages
Mazes
Word Scrambles
Word Searches
Wordoku
Words Within Words

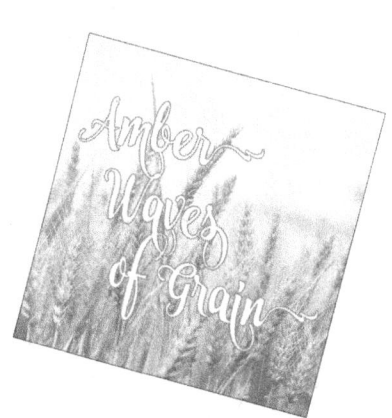

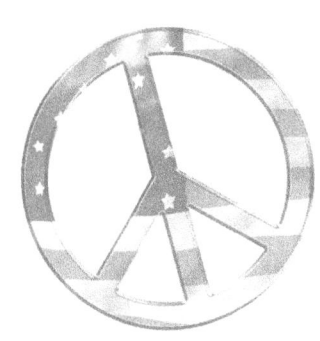

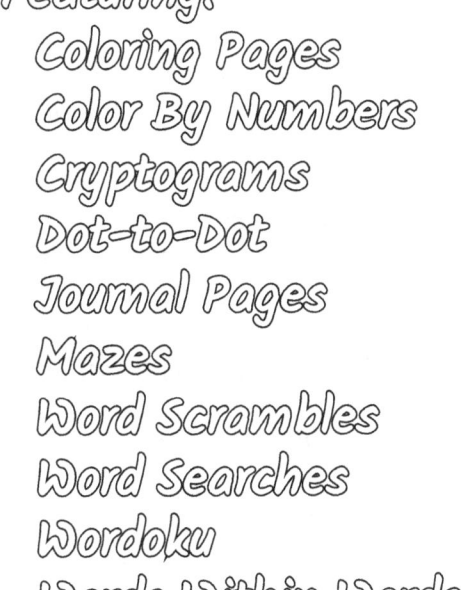

Teresa Nichole Thomas

This book is dedicated
to all the courageous
men and women
who fought
for our freedom.

Thank you!

Table of Contents

Puzzle Solutions

Instructions

Instructions
Color By Numbers

"Color by Number" designs include number markings in the areas of the drawing that are to be colored. Each number represents a certain color.

To figure out what colors correspond with the numbers, use the color key below the image, and color every area marked with that number. Continue coloring until you have colored all of the areas.

Some areas will not be marked. You can leave them white or color them with a color of your choice.

You can use colored pencils, crayons, paint, and more. For options on what you can use to color, please check out "Choose your coloring device" from the "Instructions: How To Color" section.

Instructions
Cryptograms

Using the key at the bottom of each puzzle, match the symbols in the puzzle with the key. Place the letter from the key in the blank space above each matching symbol until all blanks have been filled, as shown in the example below.

Note: Not all letters will be used in every puzzle.

W H E T H E R   Y O U   T H I N K   Y O U

C A N   O R   T H I N K   Y O U

C A N ' T ,   Y O U ' R E   R I G H T .

- H E N R Y   F O R D

☼	♫	***	☆	♠	▣	✳	◉	✦	✶	♨	❀	♫
A	B	C	D	E	F	G	H	I	J	K	L	M

♥	♇	✲	❄	◆	♮	❋	♣	❦	✿	★	✳	◗
N	O	P	Q	R	S	T	U	V	W	X	Y	Z

Instructions
Dot-to-Dot

By following the numbered dots in sequential order, you will outline an object that will "magically" be revealed once all of the dots are connected.

Starting at dot number one, draw a line to dot number two, and continue drawing the line to the numbered dot that comes next until you reach the last numbered dot.

When you are finished connecting all of the dots, you can have even more fun with the puzzle by coloring it. (For information on coloring, please see the "Instructions: How To Color" section.)

Instructions
Mazes

Find the right path through the twists and turns of each maze to reach the finish line.

Starting at the beginning of the maze, draw a line until you get to a junction (a place where you can go more than one way). Mark the junction. Look down both paths. Most of the time, you will find one path dead ends shortly thereafter. Choose the longer path, and continue drawing your line. If that path leads to a dead end, go back to the last junction you marked, and choose a different path. If that dead ends, keep working back one junction at a time, and choose a different direction until you find your way out of the maze.

Note: If you get stuck, you can try to start from the end and work your way backwards to the place where you got stuck.

Instructions
Word Scrambles

To solve word scrambles, there are a few basic things you can try:

♦ Using a separate sheet of paper, write the letters in different patterns.

♦ Alphabetize the letters.

♦ Draw a shape, like a circle, and write the letters around it. This could help you to see combinations you would not otherwise have seen.

♦ Look for word fragments and smaller words on which you can build.

♦ Look for common letter combinations, like "Q" which is almost always followed by "U".

♦ If there are a large number of consonants, look for common consonant pairs, like "sp" and "ght". If there are a lot of vowels, look for common vowel combinations, like "ea" and "ou".

♦ While many puzzles might not use them, look for common English prefixes (i.e.: dis-, sub-, re-, in-, etc.) and suffixes (i.e.: -ed, -ing, -ment, -tion, etc.). When you find a possible prefix or suffix, separate those letters from the other letters, and see what words you might be able to put together.

Instructions
Word Searches

Words in word searches can be found forward, backward, horizontally, vertically, and diagonally.

When you find a word, place a circle around the word in the grid, and cross it off the word list.

Here are some tips to help you find all of the words:

♦ Look at the puzzle as a whole, and see if any words "jump" out at you.

♦ Look at the puzzle horizontally and vertically.

♦ Scan for the first letter of a word along each row and each column.

♦ If you are nearly finished the puzzle and see that you have a space where no words have been circled, there is a good chance that some of the remaining words are hiding in that "open" space.

♦ If you are having difficulty finding a word by searching for the first letters of the word, try searching for the last letters instead.

♦ Turn the puzzle upside down.

♦ If a word in the word list includes double letters or common combinations, like "QU", try searching the grid for those.

Instructions
Wordoku

Wordoku is basically Sudoku with nine letters instead of numbers, and the rules are the same as number Sudoku.

If you do not know the basic rules of Sudoku, they are quite simple. The traditional Sudoku puzzles are made up of a simple 9 x 9 grid made up of rows, columns, and 3 x 3 "regions". Place each of the nine letters of the given word into the empty cells so that they appear only one time in each row and column. At the same time, those letters can only appear once in each region.

Columns →
Rows ↓

	O		S		R	U		
		R				M		
L		S			M	A		R
O	U			I		R	L	
				U			M	
M		L		O	A			S
R					I	S	A	
					L			

Columns →
Rows ↓

A	O	M	S	L	R	U	T	I
U	T	R	I	A	O	M	S	L
L	I	S	U	T	M	A	R	O
O	U	A	M	I	S	R	L	T
T	S	I	R	U	L	O	M	A
M	R	L	T	O	A	I	U	S
R	L	T	O	M	I	S	A	U
I	M	U	A	S	T	L	O	R
S	A	O	L	R	U	T	I	M

Instructions
Words Within Words

Using a given word, find as many words as you can with the letters in the word.

The basic rules are as follows:

♦ Not all of the letters need to be used, but words must be at least three letters long.

♦ Words must only use the letters within the word.

♦ The letters may be combined in any order.

♦ A letter may be used only as many times as it appears in the given word.

♦ Proper names and abbreviations are not allowed.

In the example below, the word "example" is used as the given word.

Example
ale
ape
lap
lax
map
pal
apex
lamp
leap
meal
palm
plea
ample
expel
maple

Instructions
How to Color

If you have not colored in many years, you might be a little unsure where to start or where to go next. Fear not. Coloring is pretty easy.

To help you get the most out of your new coloring designs, here are some suggestions about how you can get started.

Choose your coloring device

Most adults agree that when it comes to coloring, crayons just do not cut it. For more detail and shading, look for colored pencils or art pencils. Colored pencils have the added benefit of being erasable, so if you make a mistake, you can simply erase it and correct it.

Of course, you can use crayons if you desire, but they might be too wide for the tiny spaces in most adult coloring designs.

For bolder colors, try fine-tipped non alcohol-based markers or gel pens designed for art. Keep in mind, though, these could bleed through even thick paper, fabric, canvas, etc. If you are planning to use markers or pens, be sure to test them on your paper, fabric, etc., before coloring a whole design. Even if there is no bleed-through when you test your markers or pens, it can be helpful to place a blank page (or more pages, if needed) behind your designs if you want to use markers or pens.

Some other devices you can use are: pastels, watercolor pencils, tempera paint, paint pens, and charcoal. A few colorists have even been known to use glitter glue! Get wild, and use whatever adds color to your design.

Each device has its own qualities. You can combine two or more coloring devices on one design to create some really awesome and stunning effects.

Prepare your tools

The tools you choose will depend upon your chosen coloring device.

♦ If you are using colored pencils, you will need a pencil sharpener and an eraser. A colorless blending pencil, while not necessary, will help to soften the edges of your coloring. A pencil extender might also be useful for when your pencils are getting too short to be comfortably used.

♦ If you are using crayons, you will need a sharpener.

♦ If you are using markers or gel pens, make sure to have plenty of extra blank paper on hand to place behind your images to protect your surfaces and/or other coloring pages from bleed through.

♦ If you are using paint, make sure you have brushes in various sizes, especially small ones for those intricate spaces.

Choose your colors

Try not to get too hung up on using the "right" colors. Almost any color combination will work. There are no wrong colors. Experiment. Let yourself be free.

If you would rather stick to a theme, however, there are several things you could do:

♦ Spread out your chosen coloring device(s). Then just pick up a color, and start coloring.

♦ Choose colors you love. If the colors are ones you adore, then your finished design will be beautiful to you--and, really, that is all that matters. Right?

♦ Choose rainbow colors. Rainbows are a super simple choice; you already know the colors look good together.

♦ Use only cool colors or warm colors. Choosing only cool colors, like blues, greens, and purples will lend a zen effect to your coloring projects, and warm colors, like reds, oranges, and yellows will give them an air of excitement. Be sure to switch things up by using tints and shades of your chosen color temperature.

- Search online for a color scheme generator. There are plenty out there; try different ones and see which one(s) you like best.

- Search online for color trends. Pantone releases their color trends twice per year.

- Look up a painter whose work you like. Observe the palette he or she used.

- Search online for graphic design projects. Pay attention to the colors the designer used.

- Go wild! Choose colors you would never choose otherwise; you will be amazed at how gorgeous your designs can be!

Set the mood

To get the full calming effect from coloring, pour your favorite beverage, and listen to some relaxing music while you color. Create a peaceful and soothing atmosphere, and let your creative juices flow. You will soon be surprised at how much fun you are having and just how great coloring can be for stress relief.

Make it a regular habit

Coloring can help relax you and unlock your creativity. Find just a few minutes every day to color a small section, and you will see the benefits throughout the day as you become less stressed. You might even find that coloring helps you learn to be more creative in other aspects of your life, so have fun with it. Then see for yourself what happens.

Whatever you do, try to remember that mistakes happen, and coloring is meant to be relaxing--not a stressful exercise in perfection.

So, grab your favorite beverage. Put on some relaxing music. Choose your device(s). Get your tools ready. Let that stress fade away as you immerse yourself in your new America, the Beautiful Activity Book!

Activities

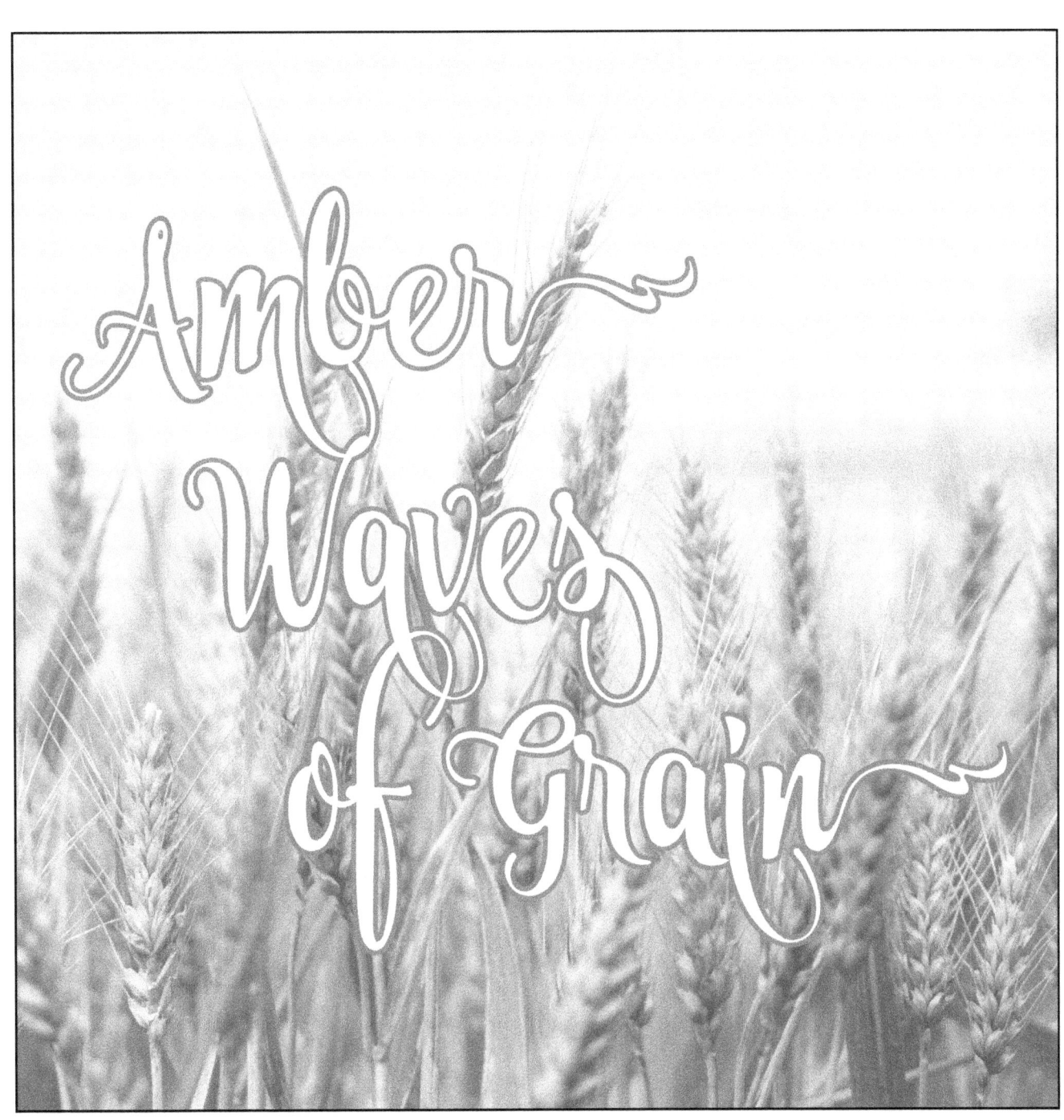

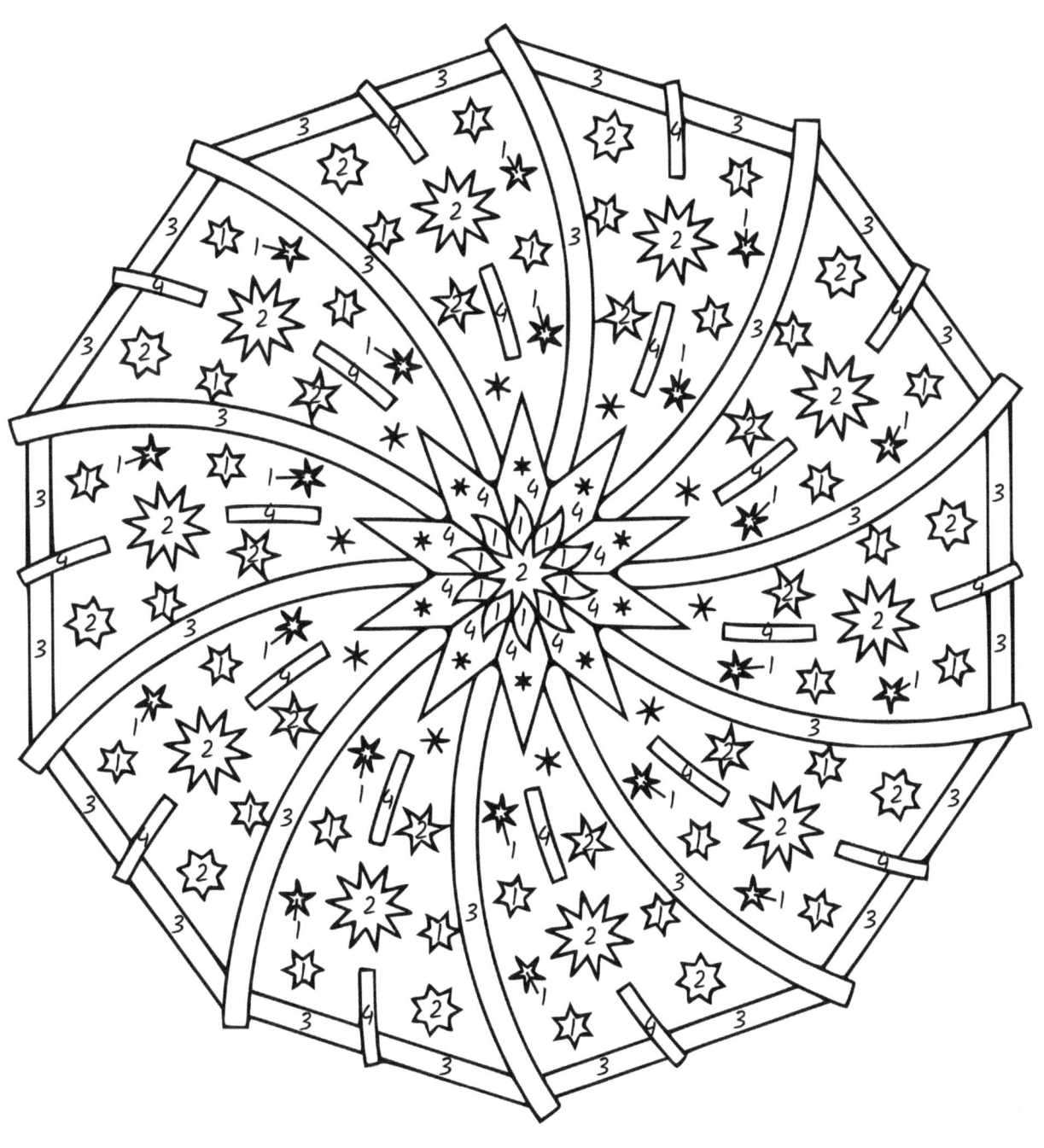

1 = Yellow
2 = Orange
3 = Red
4 = Dark Blue

_____

_____

_____

_____

_____

_____

_____

_____

_____

_____

_____

_____

                        _____

                        _____

                        _____

                        _____

                        _____

                        _____

                        _____

Maze
Statue of Liberty

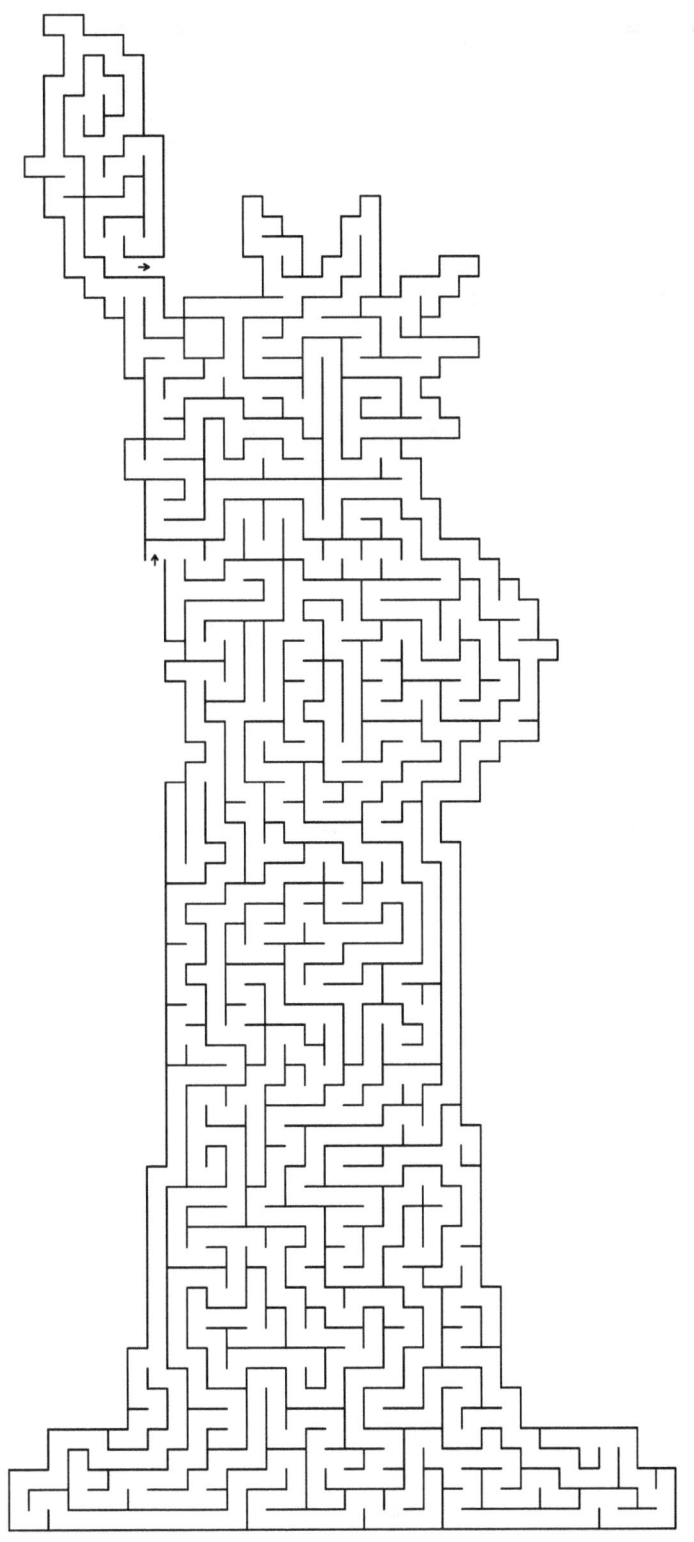

Wordoku
Sparkling

					I			
				R		N	L	P
R				N	P	A		
		G				P		
			K	I	N			
	A		R					
L						I		N
G				A	K	R		
I						G		

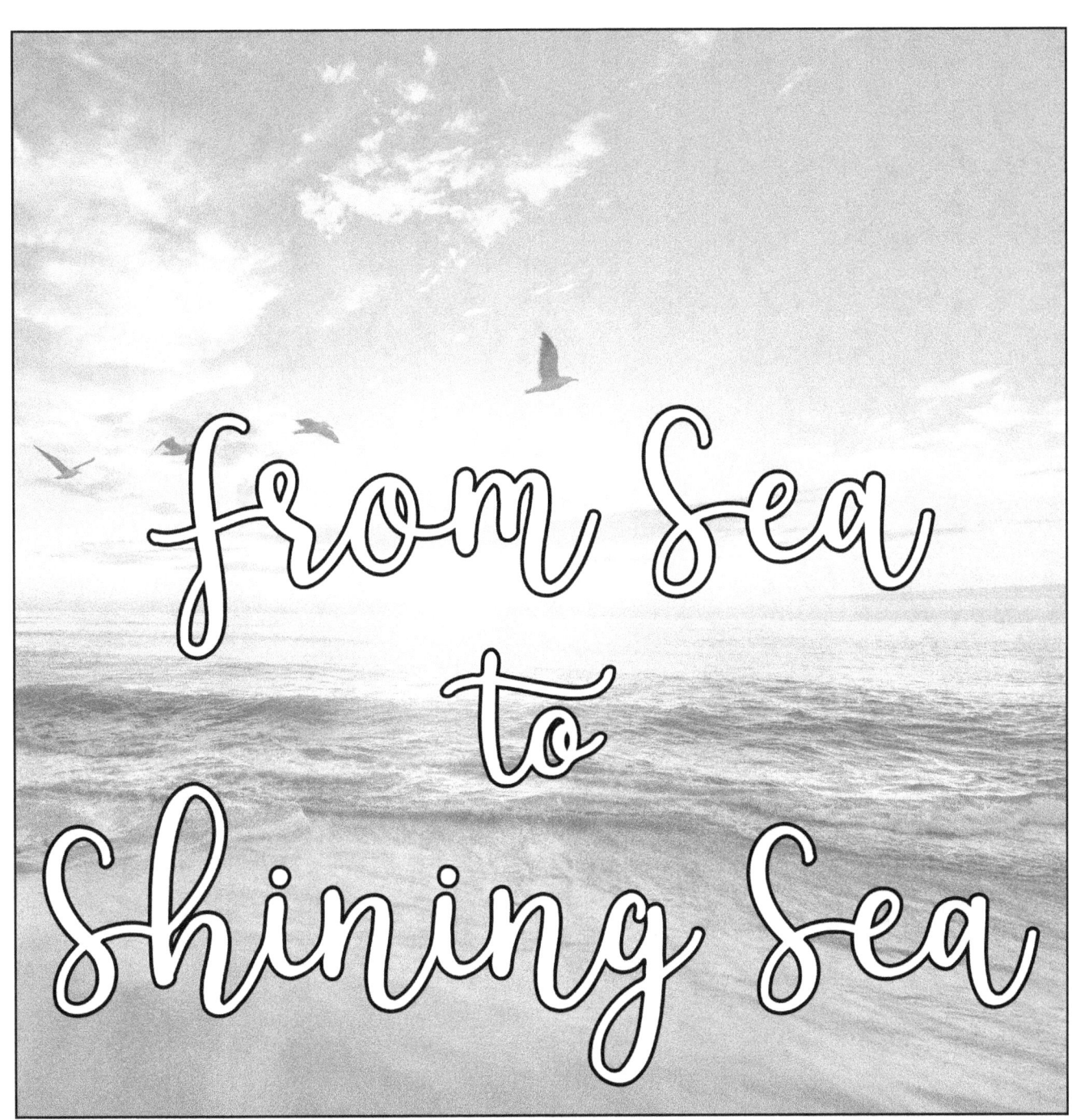

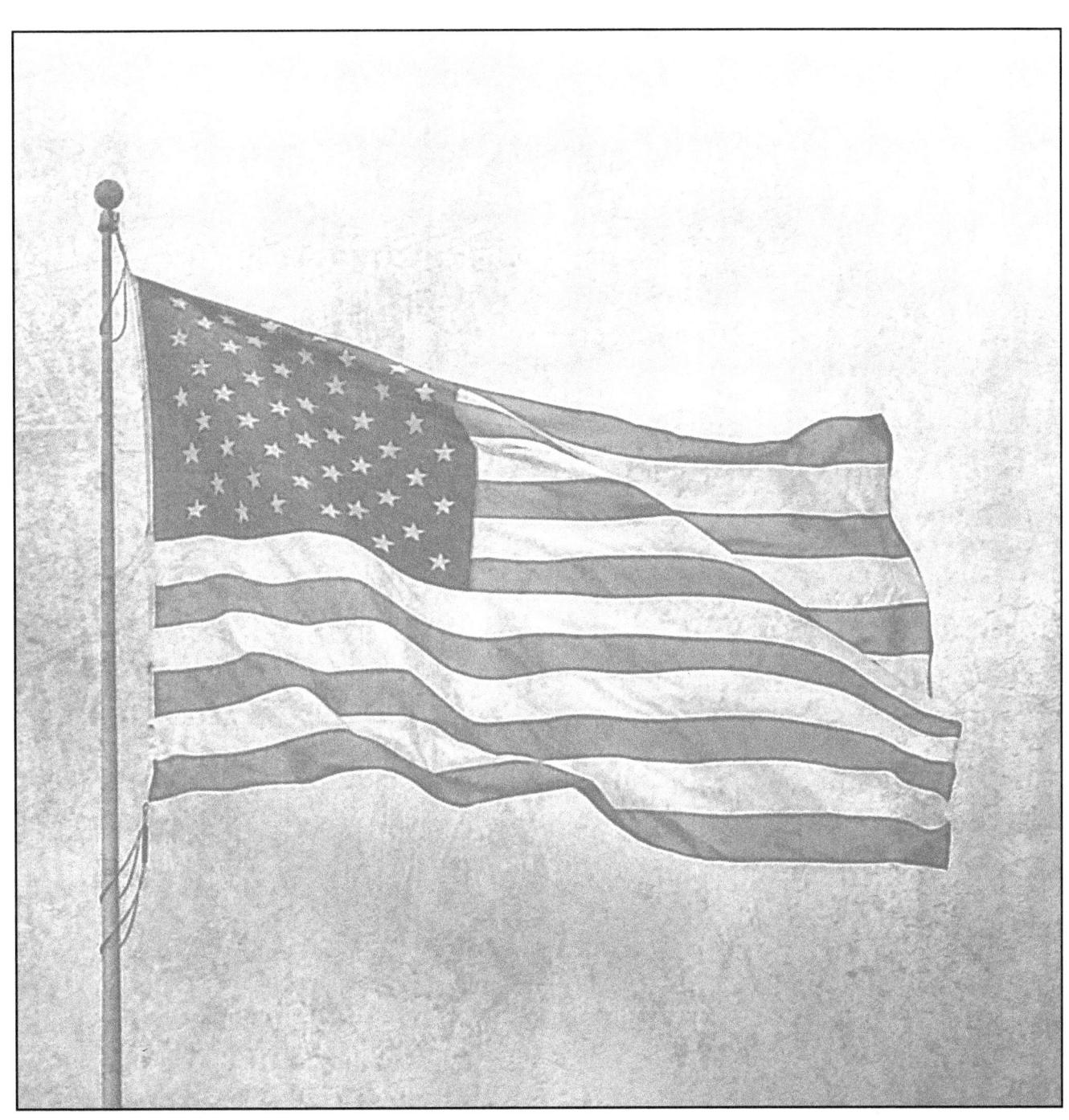

Cryptogram

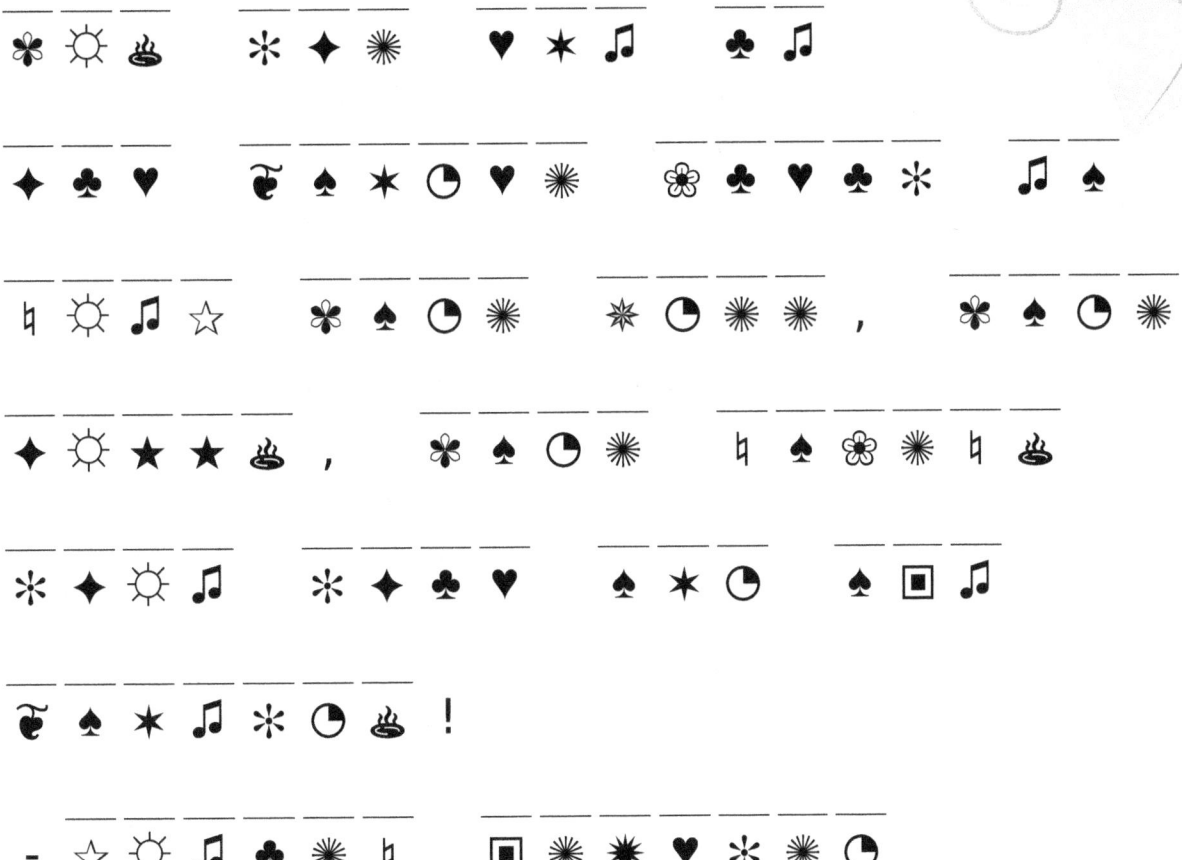

☼	✷	ℰ	☆	✴	✶	♫	◆	♣	◆	𝔤	♮	✿
A	B	C	D	E	F	G	H	I	J	K	L	M

♪	♠	★	✱	◐	♥	✳	✦	❀	▣	✺	♨	❄
N	O	P	Q	R	S	T	U	V	W	X	Y	Z

Word Search
The 50 States

Alabama	Louisiana	Ohio
Alaska	Maine	Oklahoma
Arizona	Maryland	Oregon
Arkansas	Massachusetts	Pennsylvania
California	Michigan	Rhode Island
Colorado	Minnesota	South Carolina
Connecticut	Mississippi	South Dakota
Delaware	Missouri	Tennessee
Florida	Montana	Texas
Georgia	Nebraska	Utah
Hawaii	Nevada	Vermont
Idaho	New Hampshire	Virginia
Illinois	New Jersey	Washington
Indiana	New Mexico	West Virginia
Iowa	New York	Wisconsin
Kansas	North Carolina	Wyoming
Kentucky	North Dakota	

Word Search
The 50 States

```
C T Z M I D H H M Y E B V C G U N M Q B N Z T F E
U V P S F D F A M O T T O M X L X B Z B U E Y H B
R Z I V S O W Y W A C P N H I M U J M B D P C E A
D Q A E B X S E A A B A Y L M S O A B T O X U C I
E E O T N Z P W Y E I R L E E J S M N E B F H R U
F Y J O O X D O A N J I Y I O Y H O W Q H L R U I
N S N Y A K N L A K N O A O F U B W U Y L B F B G
B T Q M W E A V C O L O R A D O I L M R X A Y H R
Y U X U Z S L D I Q S O K B Z E P Z Z I T U E I
P D X J K Y S S H E P M A R Y L A N D N U O O N V
Q Z W A S H I N G T O N N C P Q L C I O C S S Z X
B G J N O G E R O Z U N S G E O R G I A D E A F L
V K N O H A D I I Q S O A Y E S R E J E N W Z S
S E E R U D O M T T U L S M V I J T X O A N L R S
P K W T J E H I M T U K J W V P U E G I E I G D U
E K H H N O R T H D A K O T A C E R S N M M X Z T
F J A C I Y W C R O M I S S I S S I P P I U Z F M
Y A M A S S A C H U S E T T S N U V J C V M B H D
Q D P R N R D R V L W L C E G O D L H F O N O F E
M A S O O C I X E M W E N X L K V I O U J D K Y F
W V H L C V R E R O N N I A F L G Z A W B H A F W
Q E I I S S O Y M N E A W S V A V C L N K Y Y X N
K N R N I J L K O T W S M E N H B F S L A E C Y W
A R E A W B F C N A Y P N A H O L F E Q U Q C H U
O Z G B W A F U T N O J W U B M M N Q W C H I R G
W H D F R A T T R A R I Z O N A N E K O Q B P K M
L E T K F A L N Q M K N L F O I L P U Y S X R C W
Z H S L H D S E D D D Y E V U N S A Q X Z G J E A
O I N K E D M W V A G C E Z W O T G Q Z Z A
R F D W R Q C B A W P O S A S N A K F A X P B L I
```

Words Within Words
Bravery

How many words can you make from the word "bravery?"

_____ _____ _____

_____ _____ _____

_____ _____ _____

_____ _____ _____

_____ _____ _____

_____ _____ _____

_____ _____ _____

_____ _____ _____

_____ _____ _____

_____ _____ _____

_____ _____ _____

_____ _____ _____

_____ _____ _____

_____ _____

_____ _____

_____

_____

_____

_____

_____

_____

_____

_____

_____

_____

_____

_____

_____

_____

_____

_____

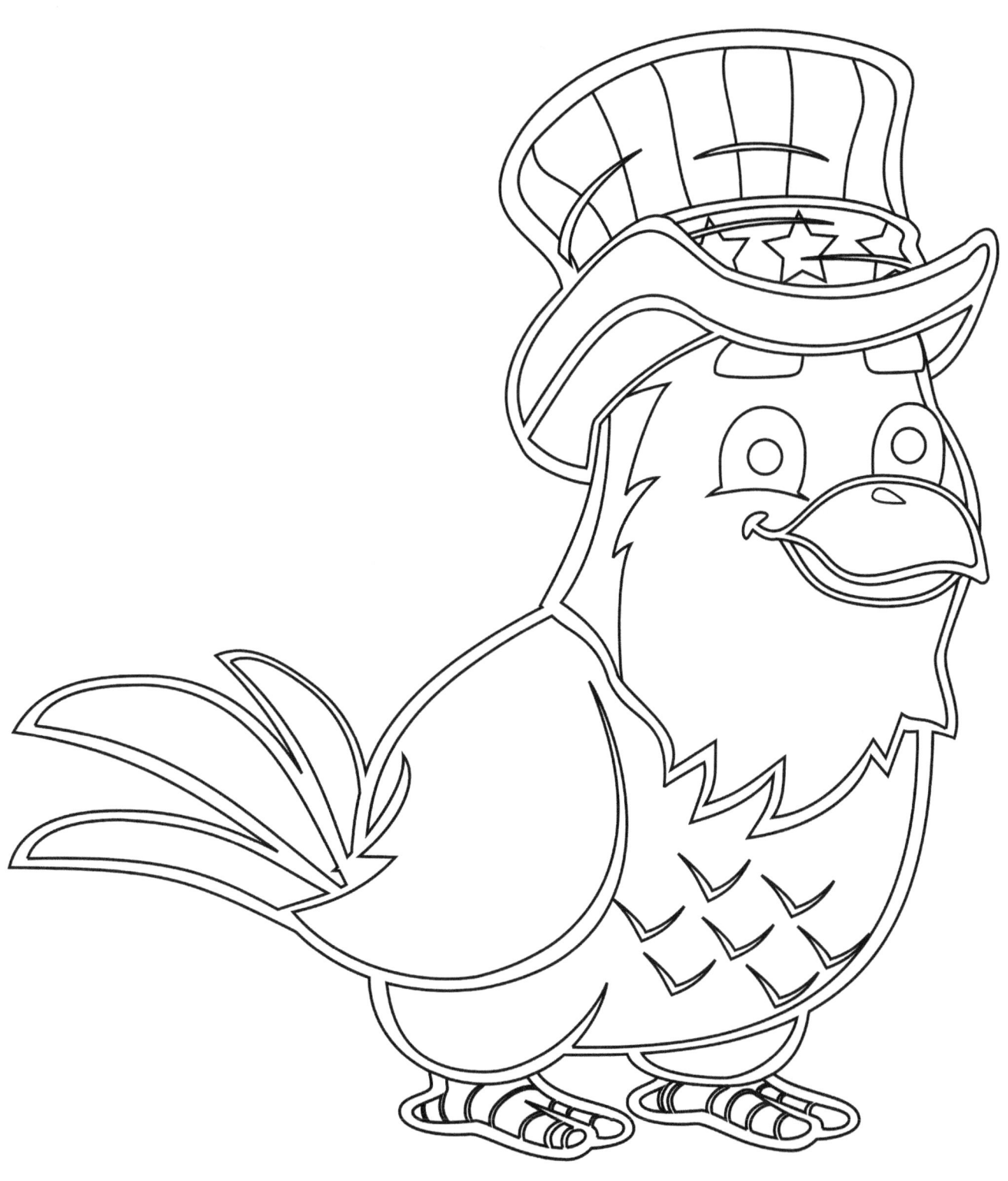

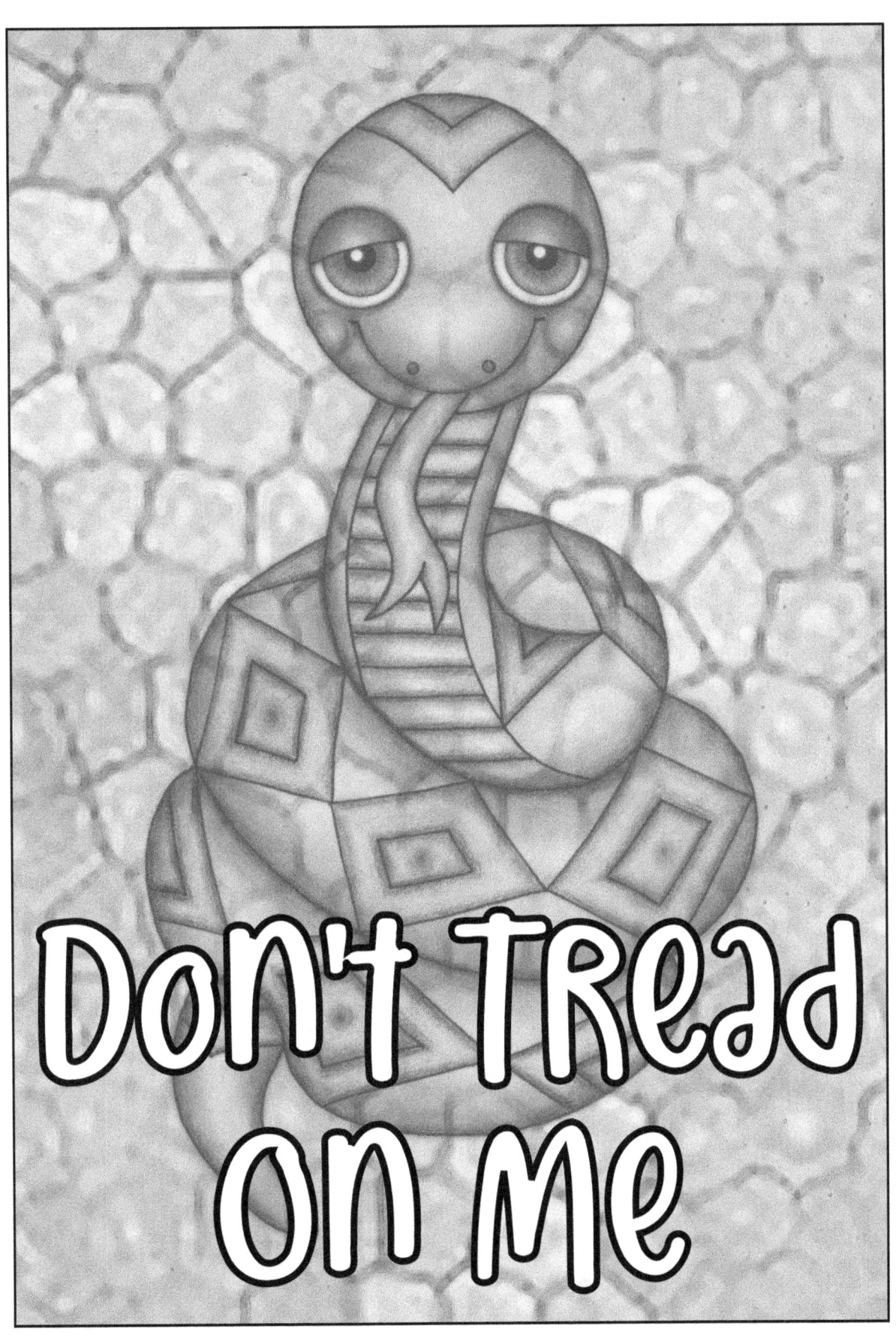

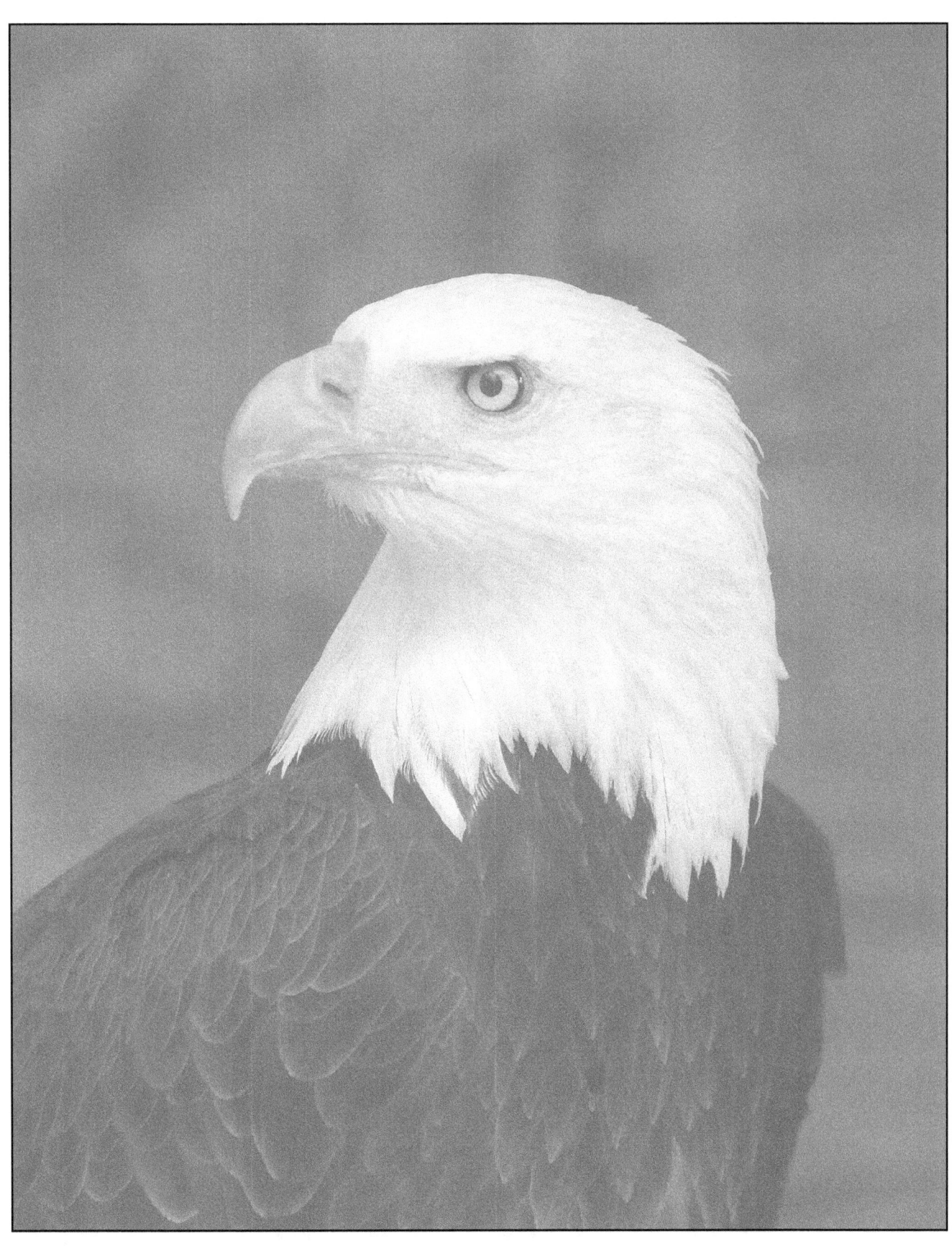

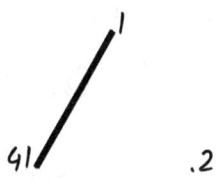

.1

41. .2

40. .3

39. .4

38. .5

37. .6

36. .7

35. .8

34. .9

33. .10

32. .11
31. .12

30. 29. .14 .13

28. .15

27. .16

26. .17

25. .18

24. .19

23. .20

22. .21

Wordoku
Welcoming

E	N				I			W
		L						
I			N				E	G
		N	G			O	C	E
G			I					
O	C			L		G		
	W			C				L
								N
	L					W		

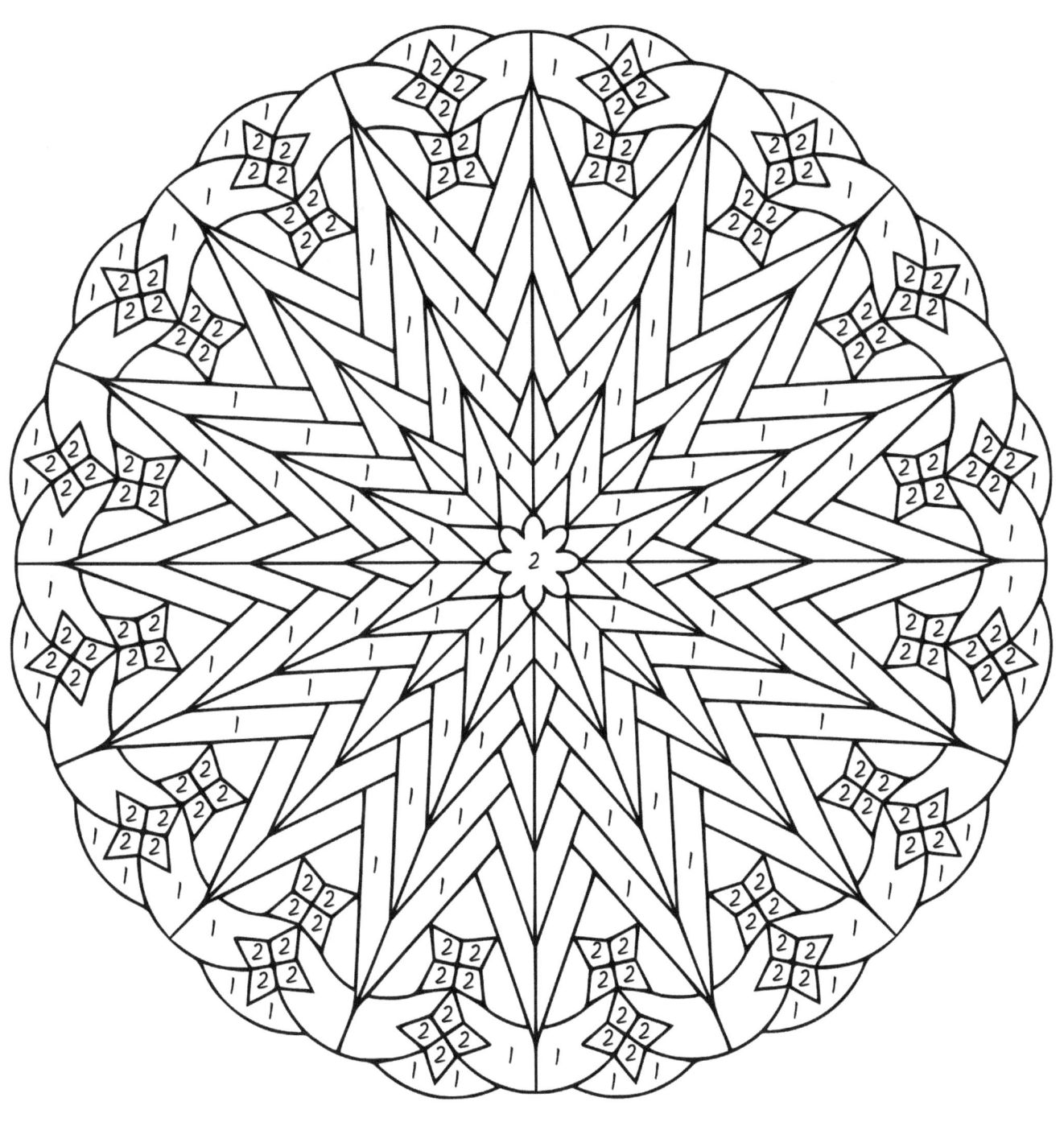

1 = Red
2 = Dark Blue

Maze
Rocket

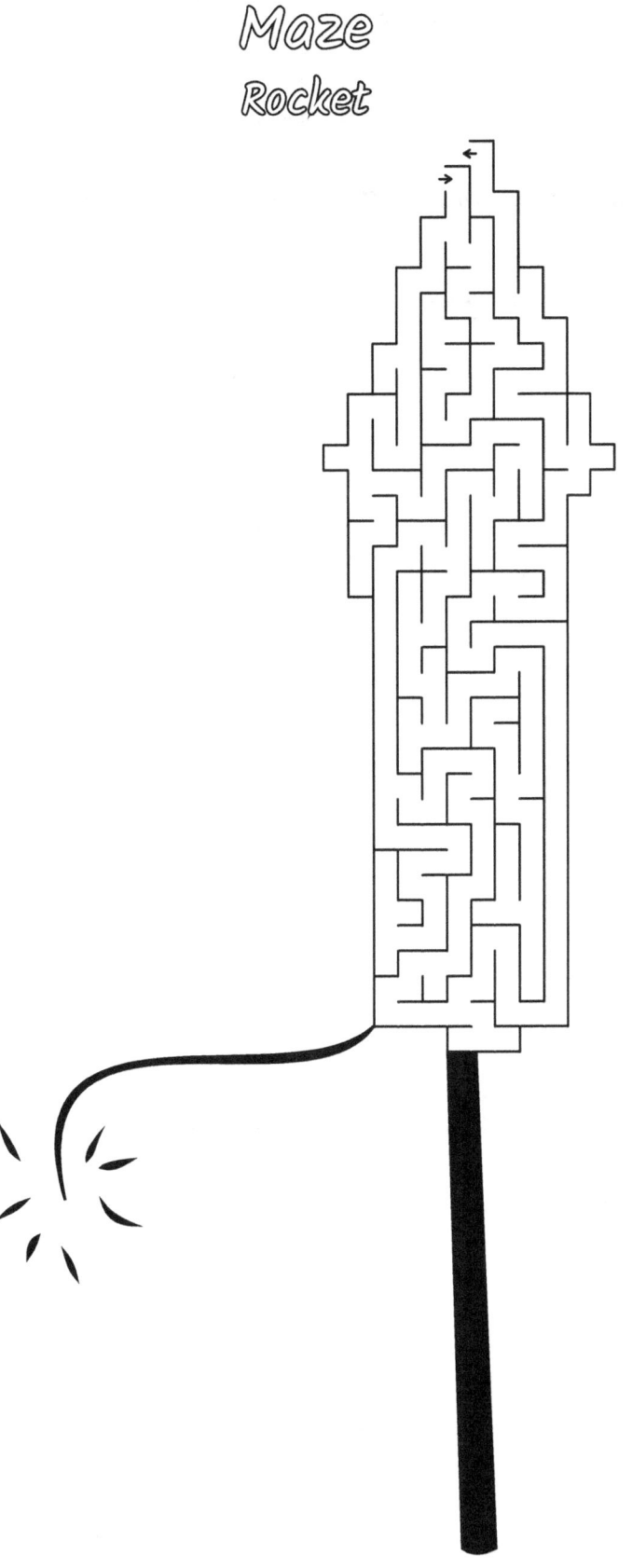

Words Within Words
Freedom

How many words can you make from the word "freedom?"

_____   _____   _____

_____   _____   _____

_____   _____   _____

_____   _____   _____

_____   _____   _____

_____   _____   _____

_____   _____   _____

_____   _____   _____

_____   _____   _____

_____   _____   _____

_____   _____   _____

_____   _____   _____

_____   _____

_____   _____

_____   _____

_____

let
FREEDOM
Ring

_____

_____

_____

_____

_____

_____

_____

_____

_____

_____

_____

_____

_____

_____

_____

_____

_____

_____

_____

_____

_____

_____

_____

_____

_____

_____

_____

_____

_____

_____

_____

_____

_____

_____

_____

_____

_____

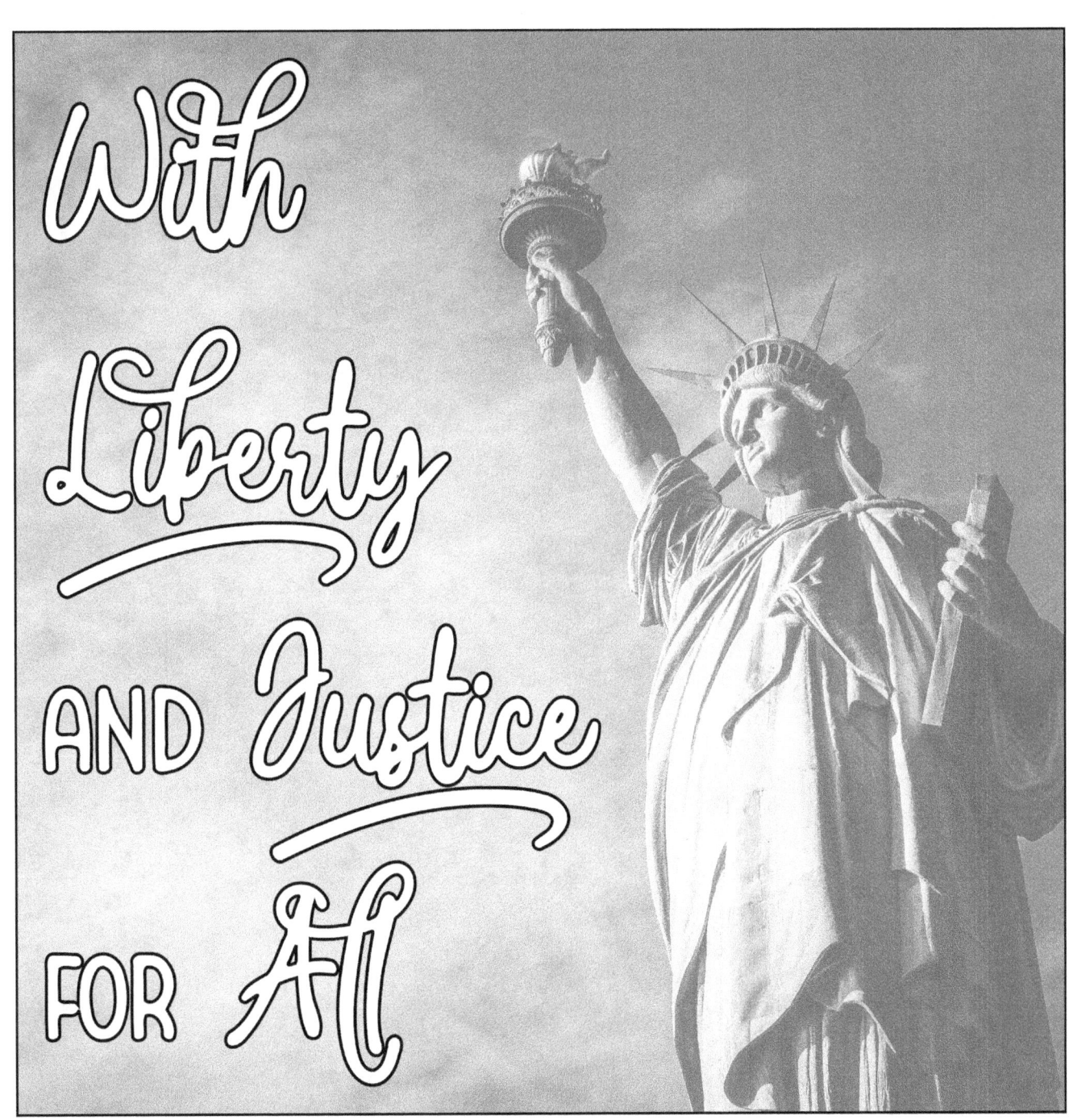

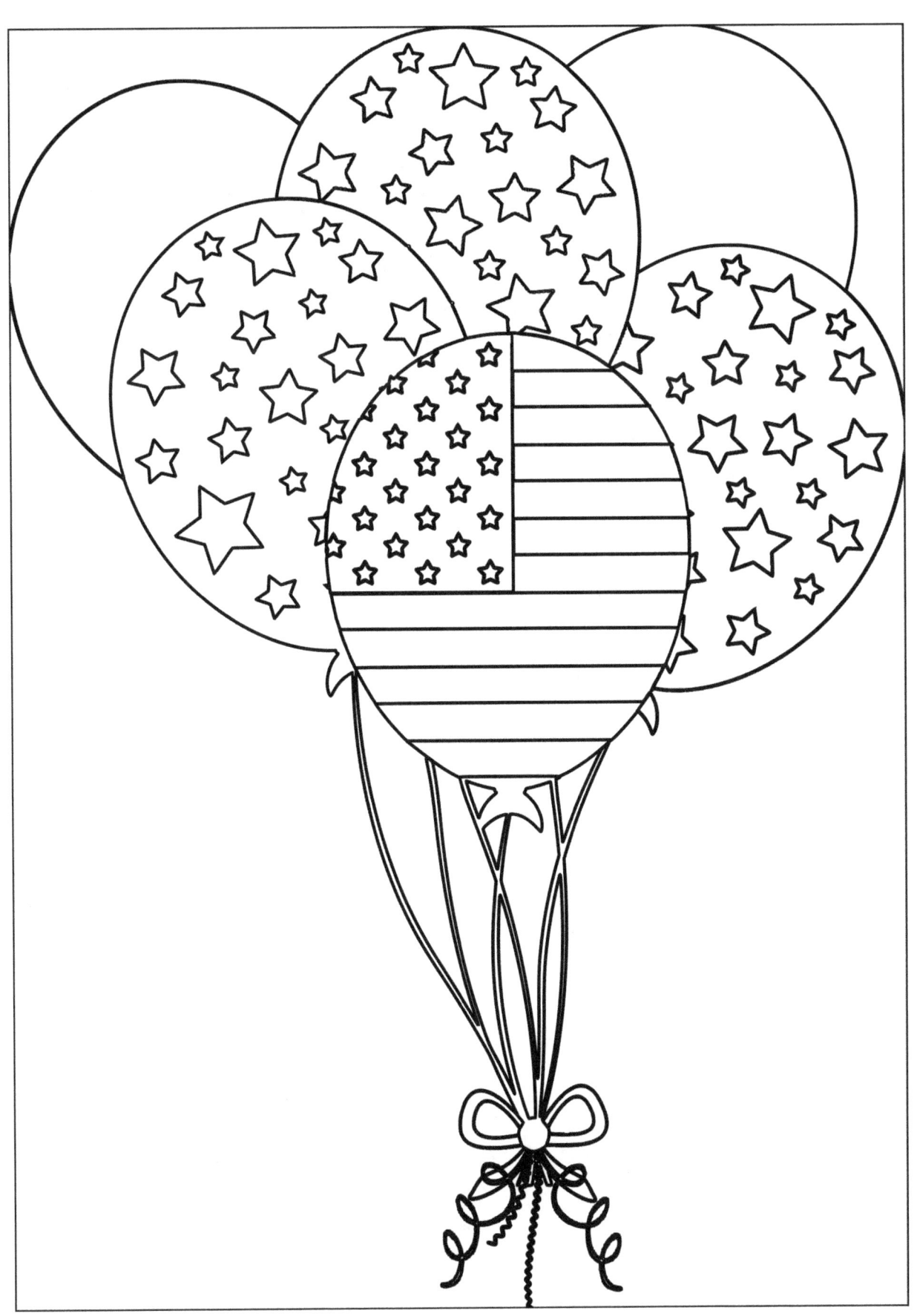

Cryptogram

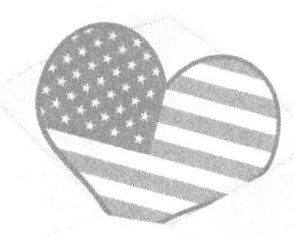

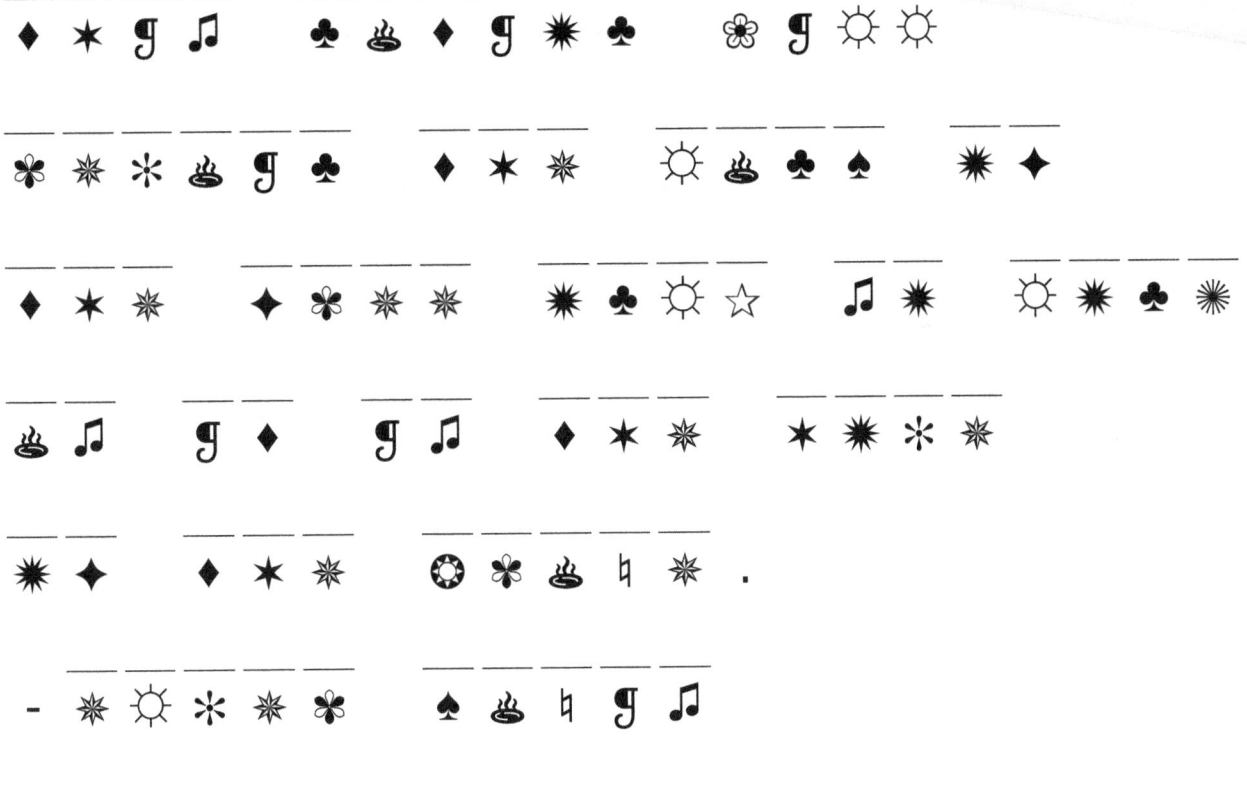

The decoder key (symbols correspond to the letters below):

A	B	C	D	E	F	G	H	I	J	K	L	M

N	O	P	Q	R	S	T	U	V	W	X	Y	Z

Word Scramble
July 4th Celebration

Unscramble the following words.

aburcbee _____

eelpipap _____

omewrtlnea _____

baietoencrl _____

amomerteocm _____

naoioedcrt _____

fvtilesa _____

srkceraefcir _____

ghnariegt _____

iegyttlr _____

msicu _____

pihenslew _____

prasrksle _____

oreksct _____

erevecren _____

remrsatse _____

Maze
Star

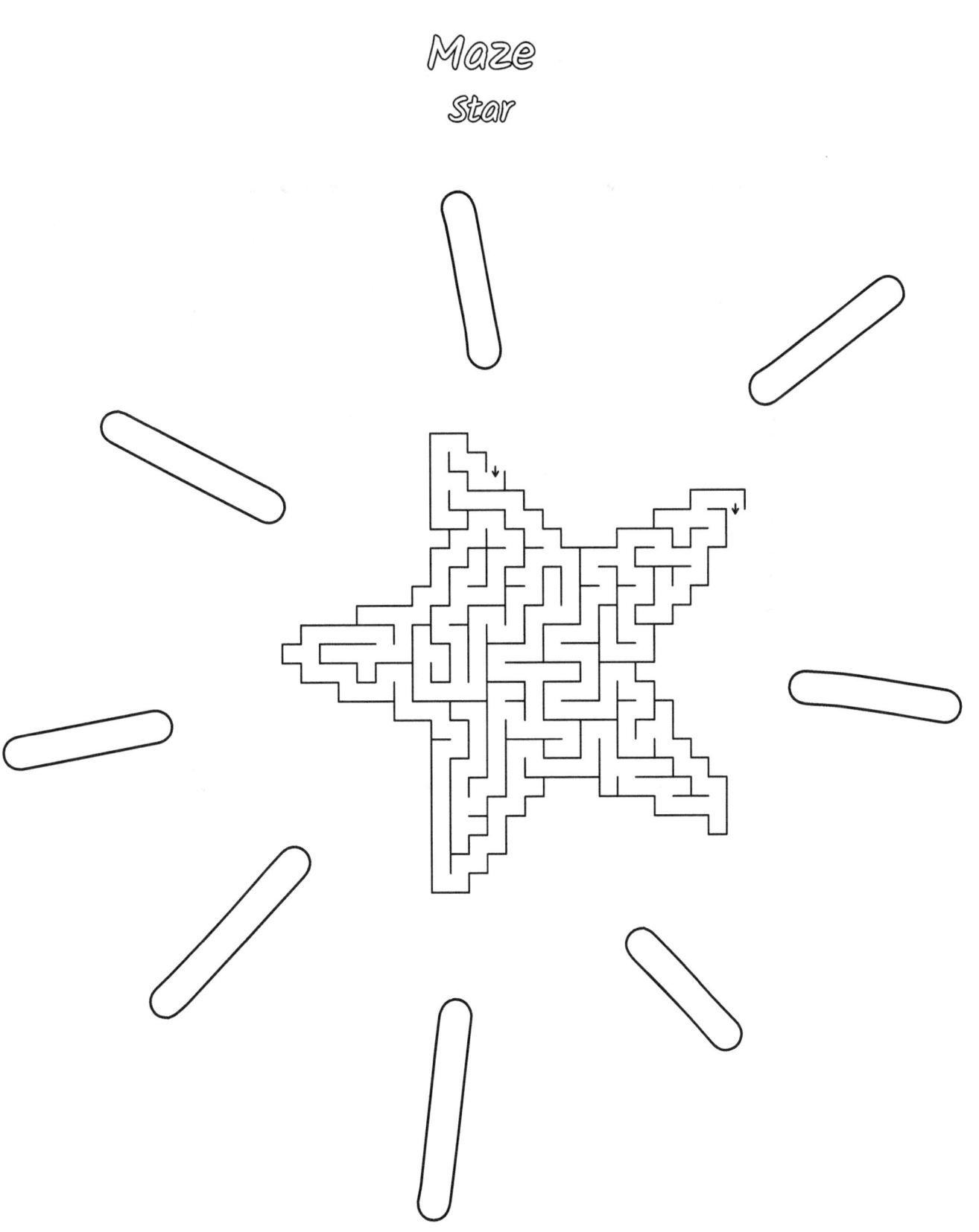

Wordoku
Wonderful

	D							
L	N	D	O	E				
		R						
		N	E		R			
		W	L	O	F			E
N				L				
	E							D
W	R	O	N	D				
	L				W			

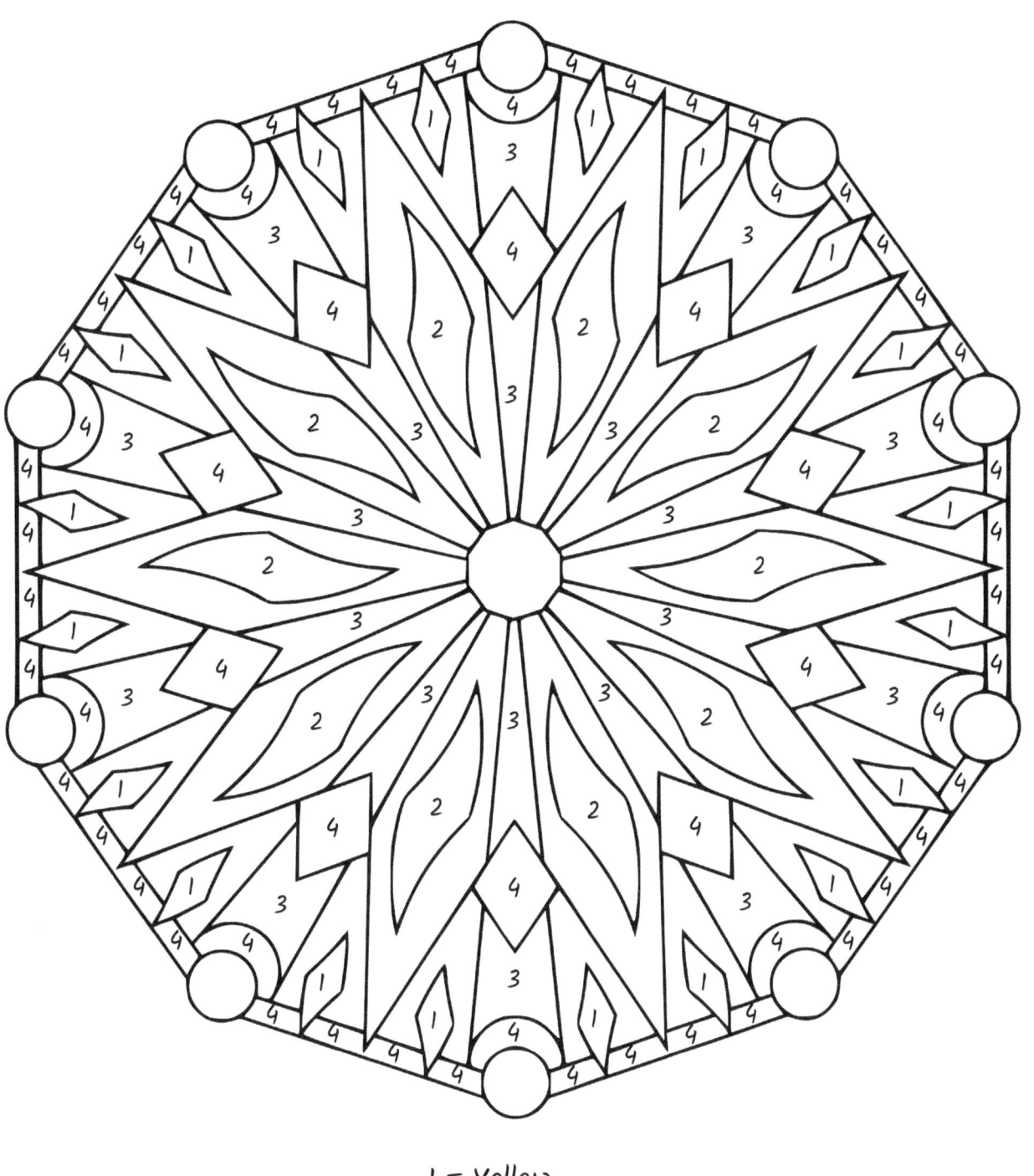

1 = Yellow
2 = Orange
3 = Red
4 = Dark Blue

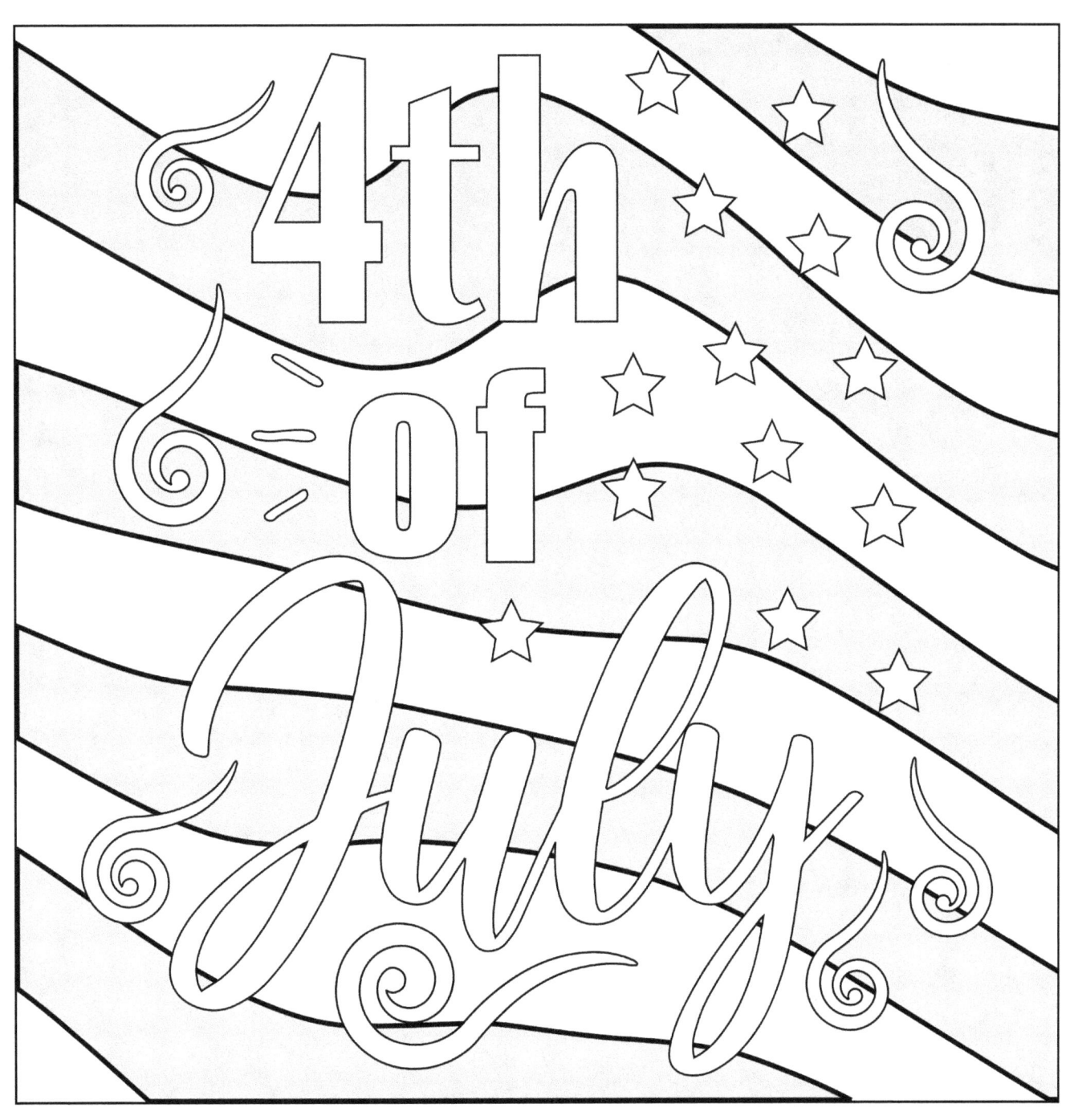

Words Within Words
Liberty

How many words can you make from the word "liberty?"

_____   _____   _____

_____   _____   _____

_____   _____   _____

_____   _____   _____

_____   _____   _____

_____   _____   _____

_____   _____   _____

_____   _____   _____

_____   _____   _____

_____   _____   _____

_____   _____   _____

_____   _____

_____   _____

_____   _____

_____   _____

Word Search
US Presidents

(George) Washington

(John) Adams

(Thomas) Jefferson

(James) Madison

(James) Monroe

(John Quincy) Adams

(Andrew) Jackson

(Martin) Van Buren

(William Henry) Harrison

(John) Tyler

(James K.) Polk

(Zachary) Taylor

(Millard) Fillmore

(Franklin) Pierce

(James) Buchanan

(Abraham) Lincoln

(Andrew) Johnson

(Ulysses S.) Grant

(Rutherford B.) Hayes

(James) Garfield

(Chester) Arthur

(Grover) Cleveland

(Benjamin) Harrison

(Grover) Cleveland

(William) McKinley

(Theodore) Roosevelt

(William Howard) Taft

(Woodrow) Wilson

(Warren G.) Harding

(Calvin) Coolidge

(Herbert) Hoover

(Franklin D.) Roosevelt

(Harry S.) Truman

(Dwight) Eisenhower

(John F.) Kennedy

(Lyndon B.) Johnson

(Richard) Nixon

(Gerald) Ford

(Jimmy) Carter

(Ronald) Reagan

(George) Bush

(Bill) Clinton

(George W.) Bush

(Barack) Obama

(Donald) Trump

Word Search
US Presidents

```
Z M I I P O K E N N E D Y Y M T H M T
E C H G C P M A X T I T D B K N H A G
Q K C R J M M E S N S O L R O S R D J
T I L A K U Z Y C I E M E X U T E A K
U N C N R R C O T D N H I B H G V M K
J L O T H T O L D N H N F U H G O S G
X E B S T L E V E S O O R C S R O M I
I Y M Y I V G R U V W T A H E T H A J
V X M D E R U B O Z E Q G A D S A D O
Y L G S C B R H J M R L G N I D R A H
Z E O R N O M A A U L A A A I E R X N
T O B A M A C J H Y N L P N L H I O S
R Y V V C K T F A T E I I Y D N S T O
M A D I S O N F O V E S T F O N O A N
H H P O J E F F E R S O N S H Q N Y W
D Y N O T N I L C E D N L O C N I L Y
P K U A L Z C E A Z D I J T D A V O O
H H M Q B K S B T U W L A D L F S R X
```

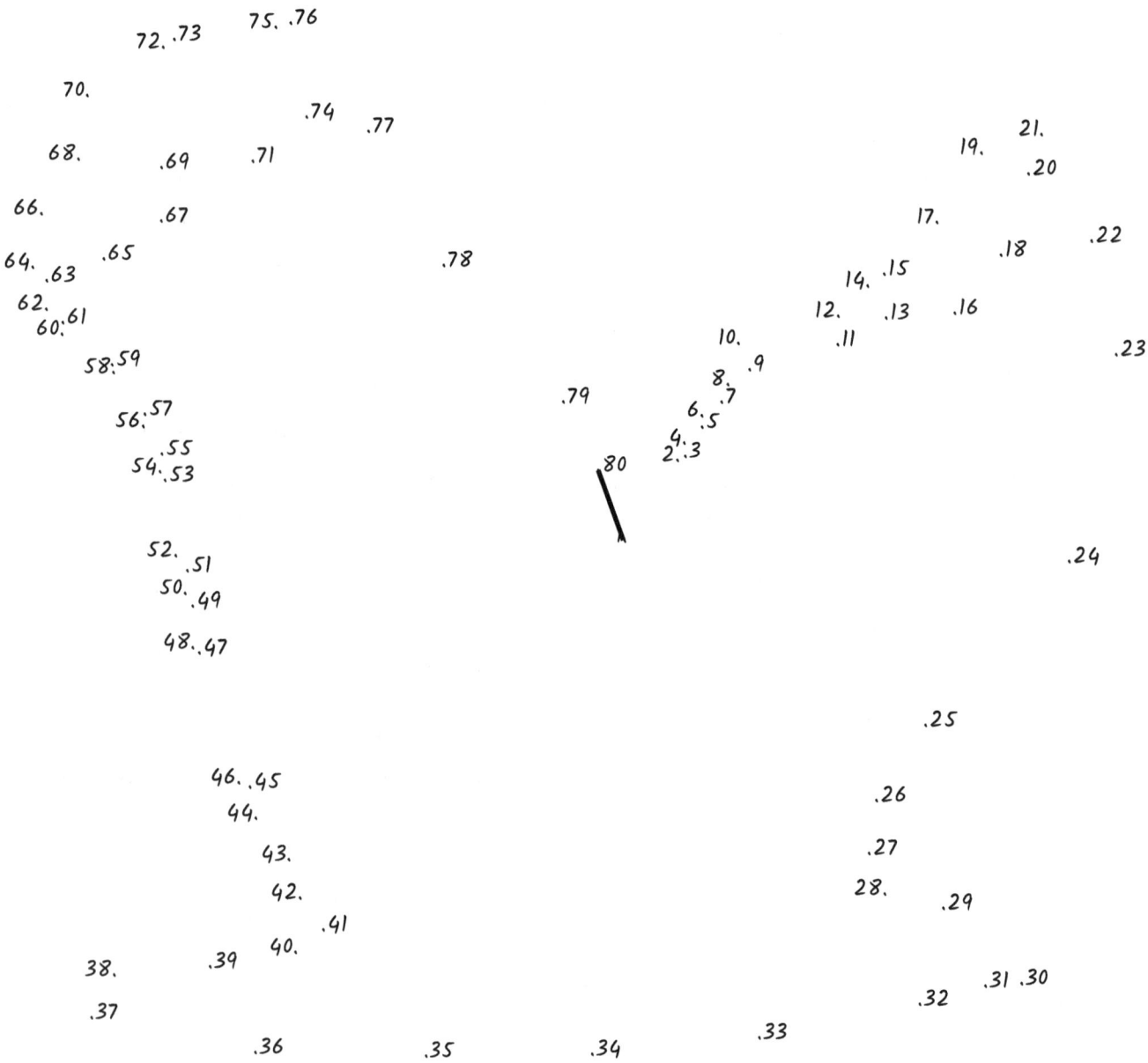

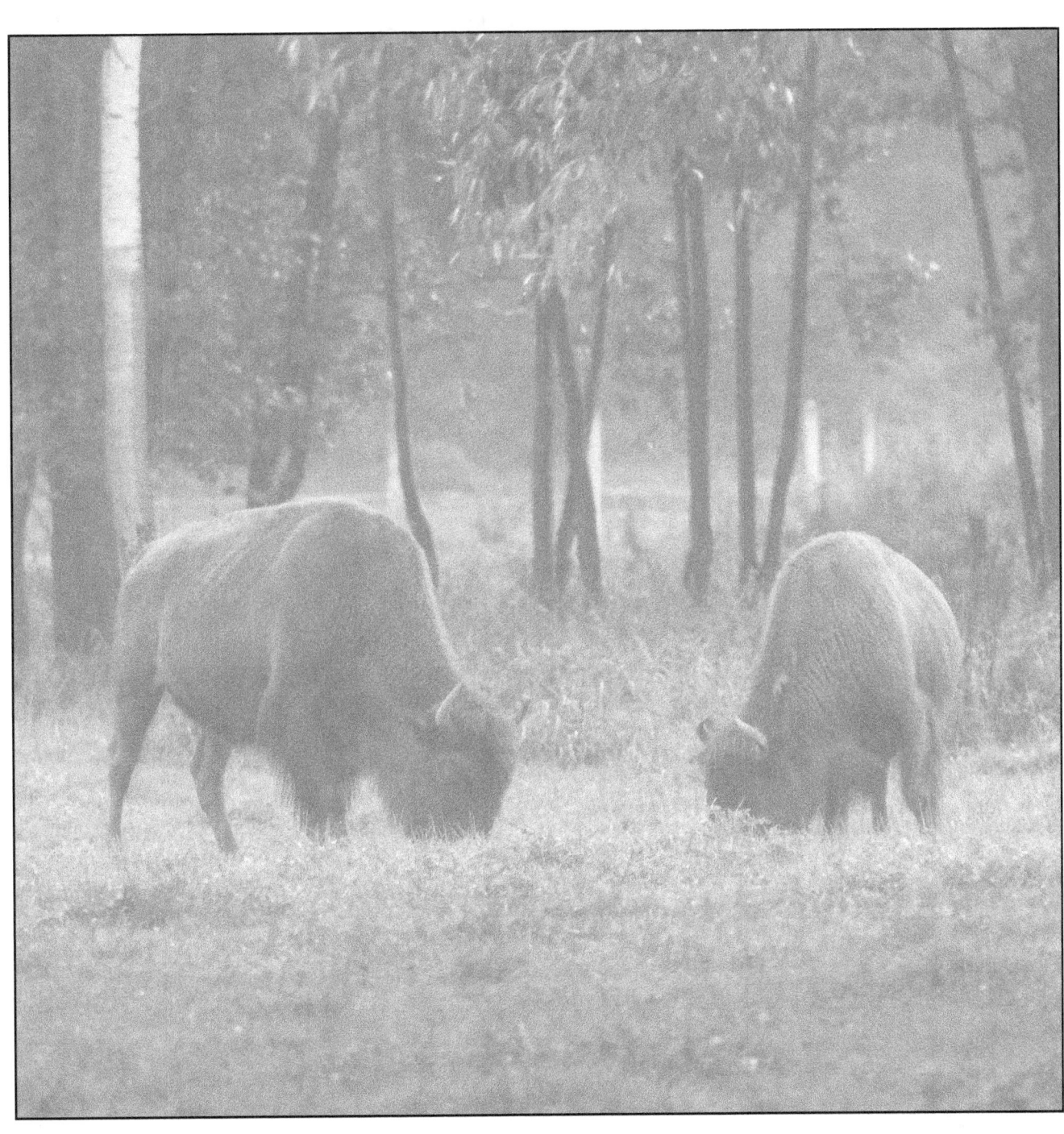

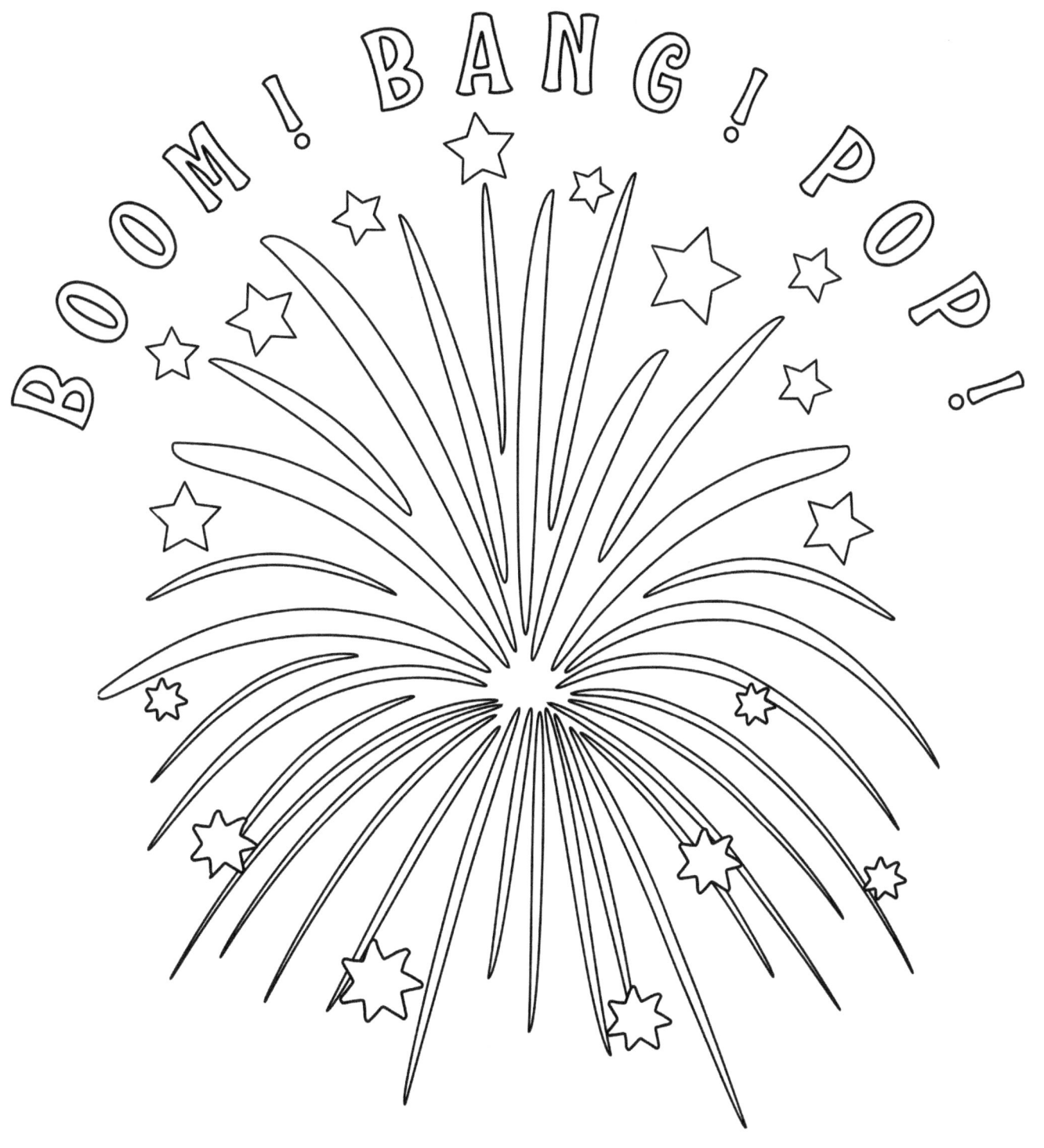

Cryptogram

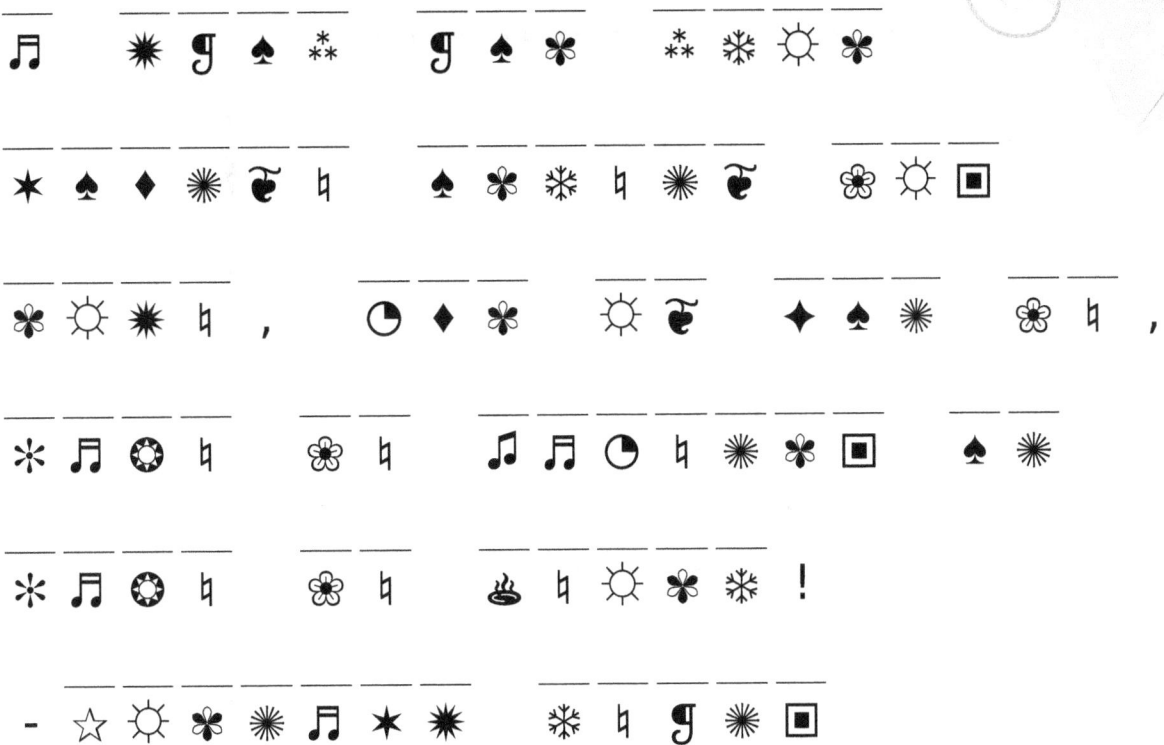

☼	◐	★	♨	♮	◆	✳	❄	♪	✹	✸	♫	❀
A	B	C	D	E	F	G	H	I	J	K	L	M

ℊ	♠	☆	★	✳	ℰ	✿	◆	◉	✳	♣	▣	♥
N	O	P	Q	R	S	T	U	V	W	X	Y	Z

Wordoku
Coastline

		T				N	O	
				N	A		S	I
		I	T	C		O	A	
L						C		
	N	C		S	O		T	
			I		N			
	S	N			T			

_____

_____

_____

_____

_____

_____

_____

_____

_____

_____

_____

_____

_____

_____

_____

AMERICA

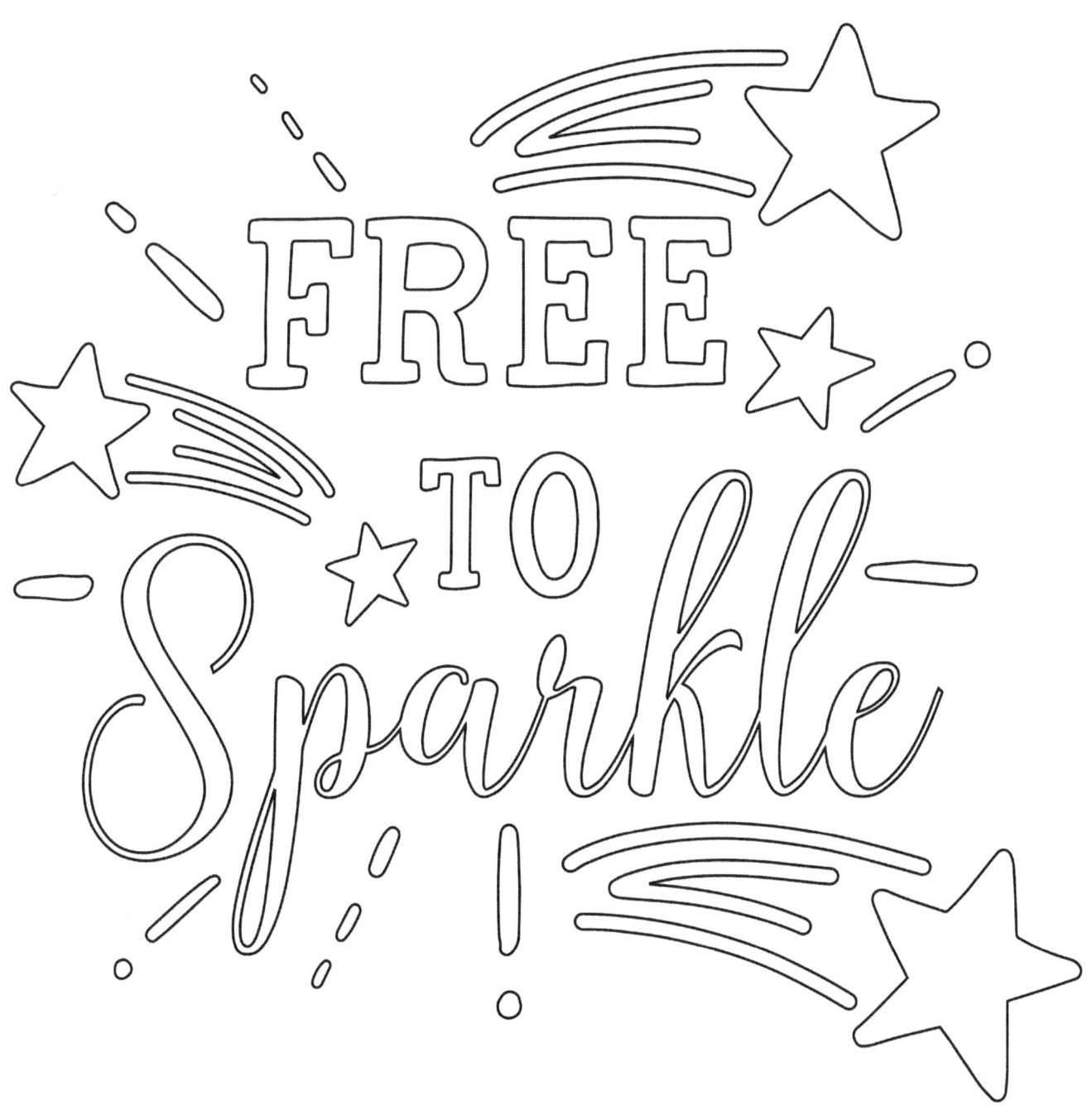

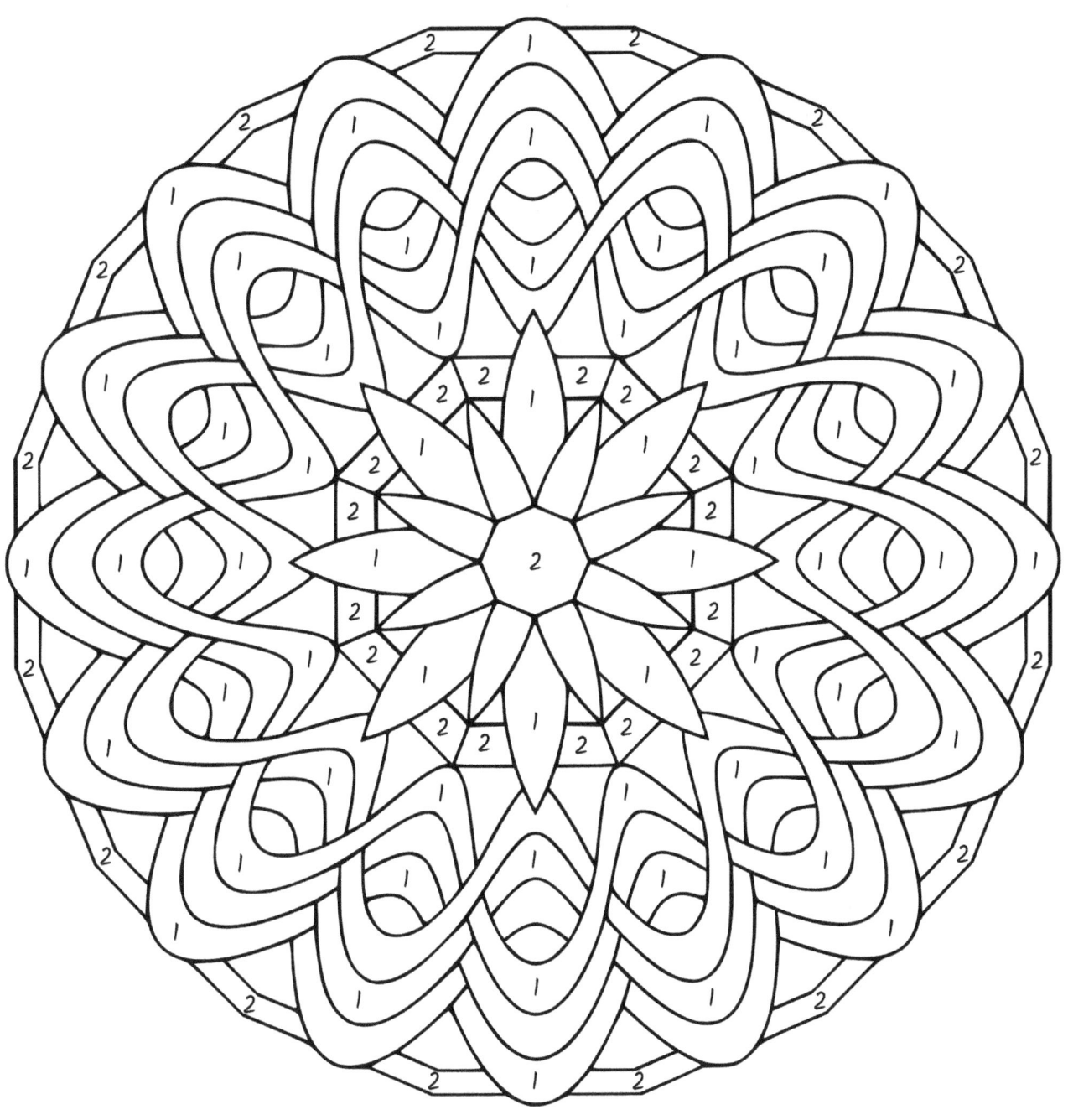

1 = Red
2 = Dark Blue

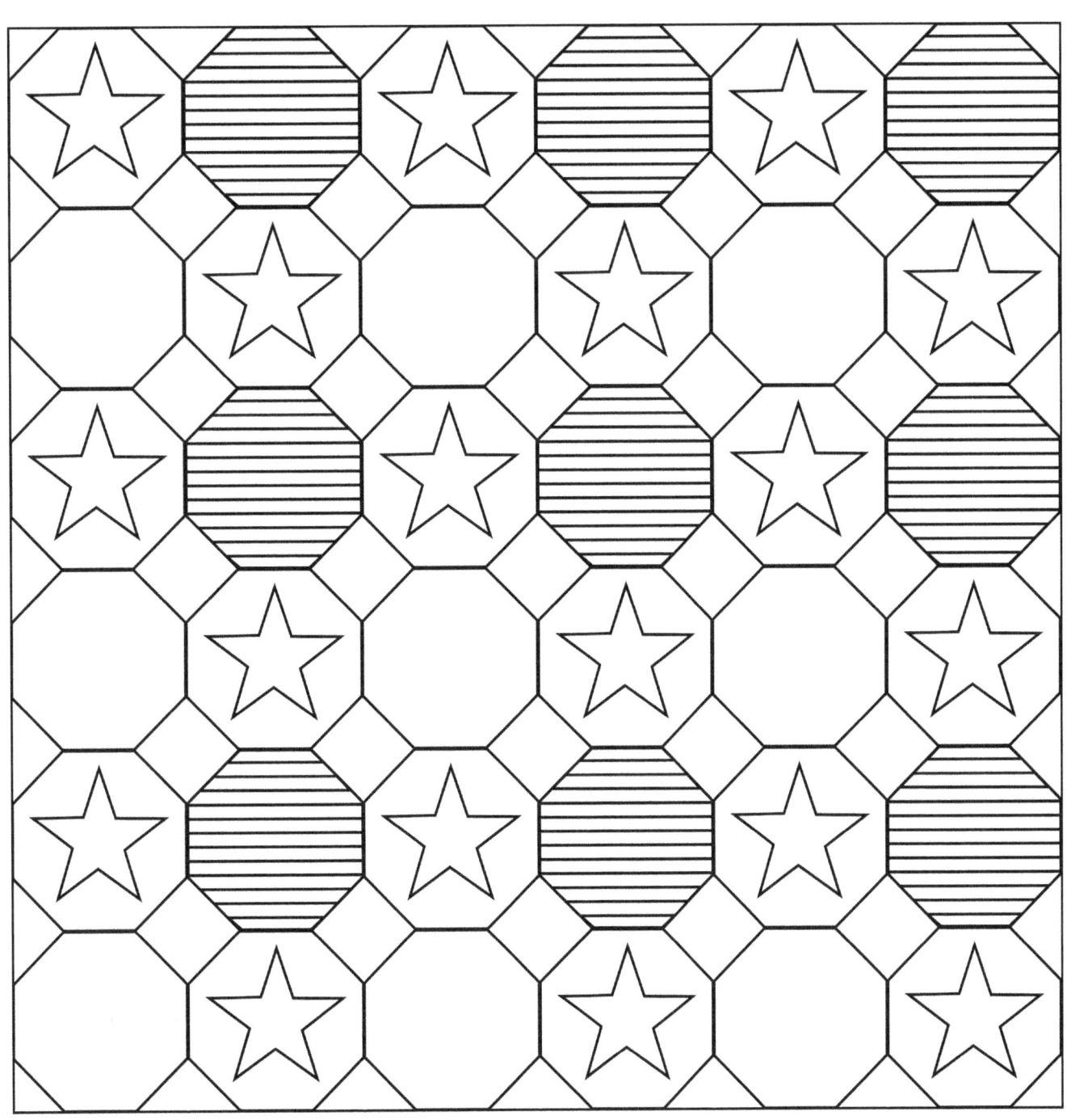

Maze
Eagle

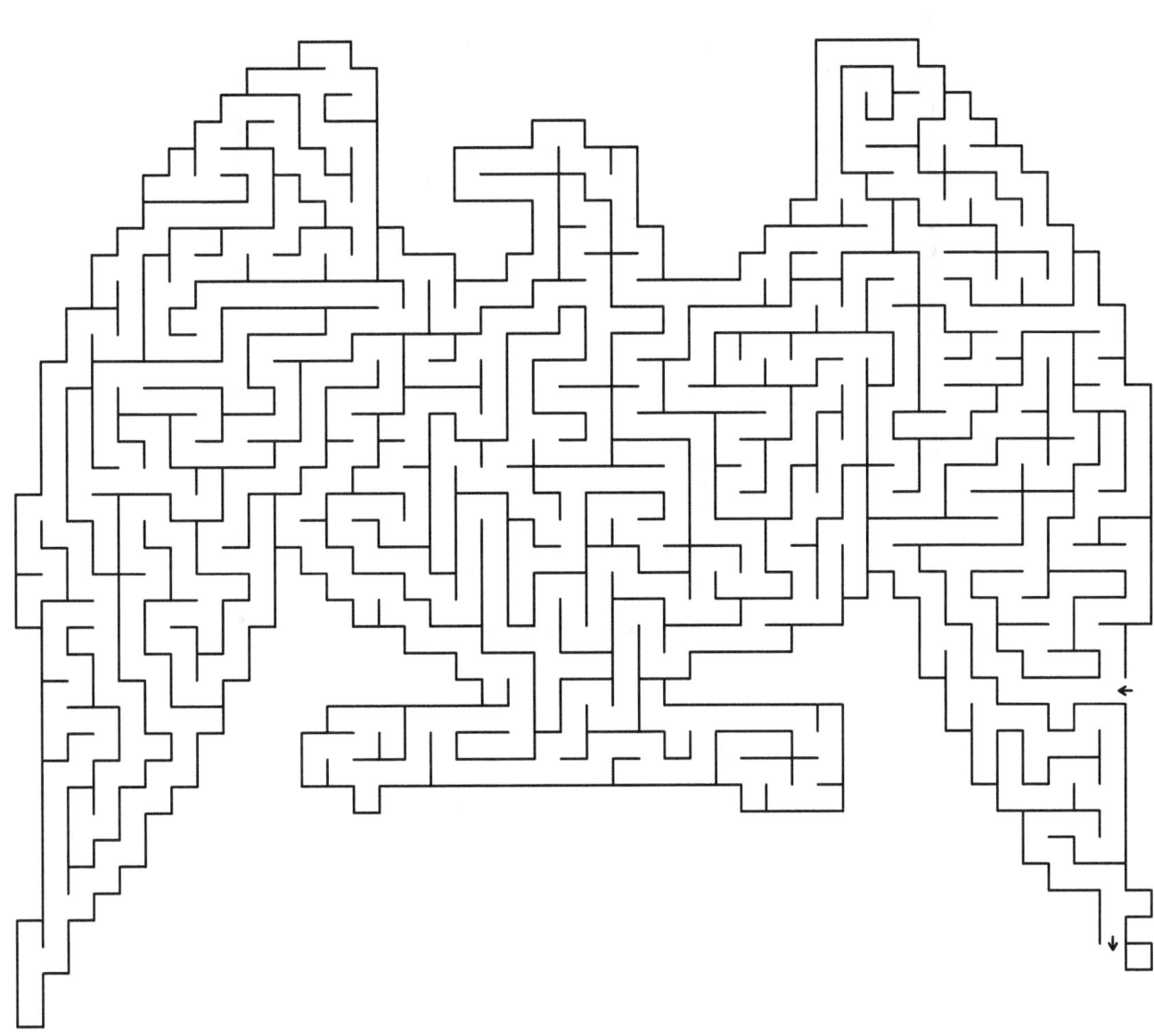

Wordoku
Discovery

R		O					C	E
		C						R
	Y	R	C			I		
V		E	O		Y			
			D					O
					O		V	
I	V		E					
		Y	R		C			I

_____

_____

_____

_____

_____

_____

_____

_____

_____

_____

_____

_____

_____

_____

_____

_____

_____

_____

_____

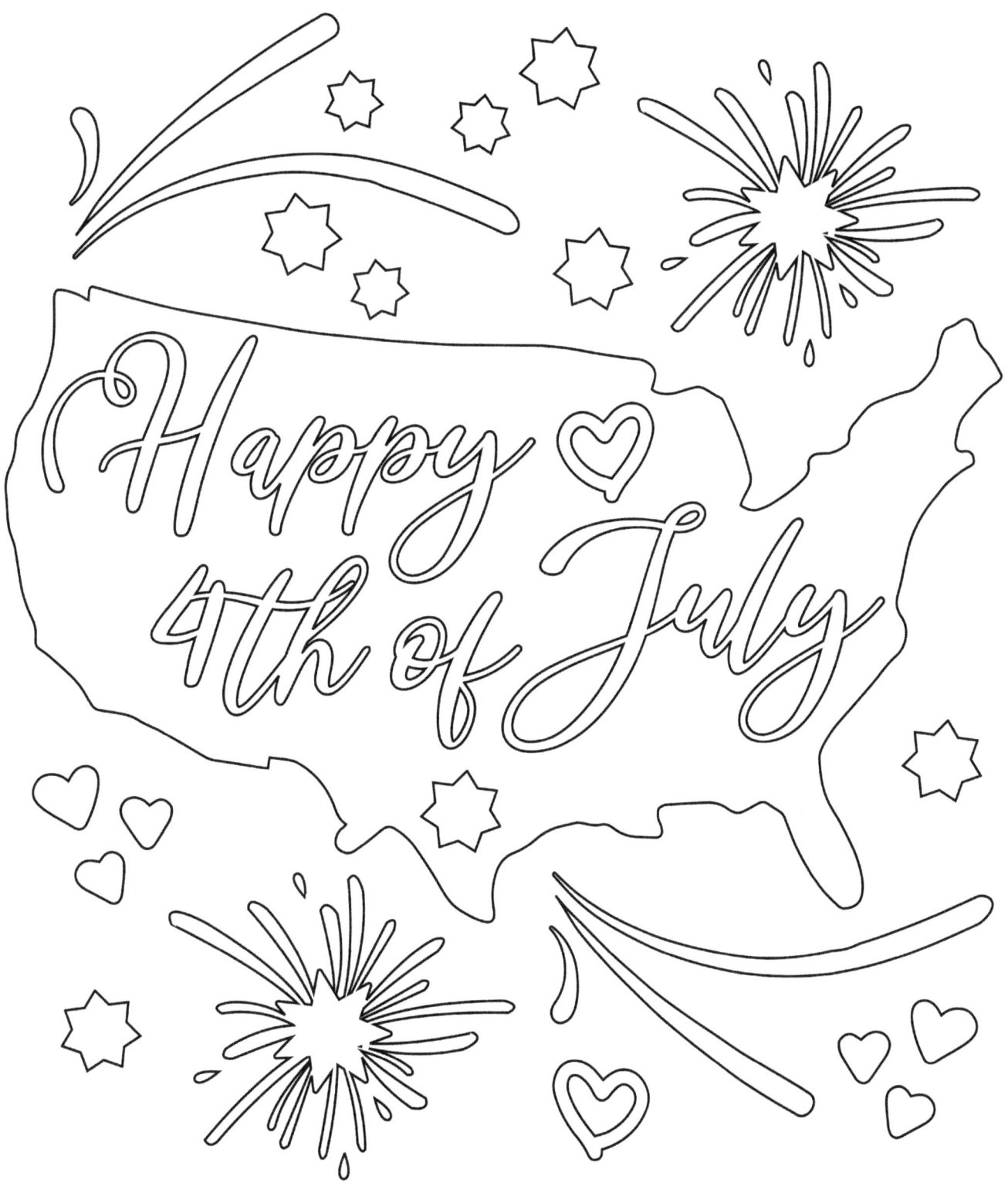

Cryptogram

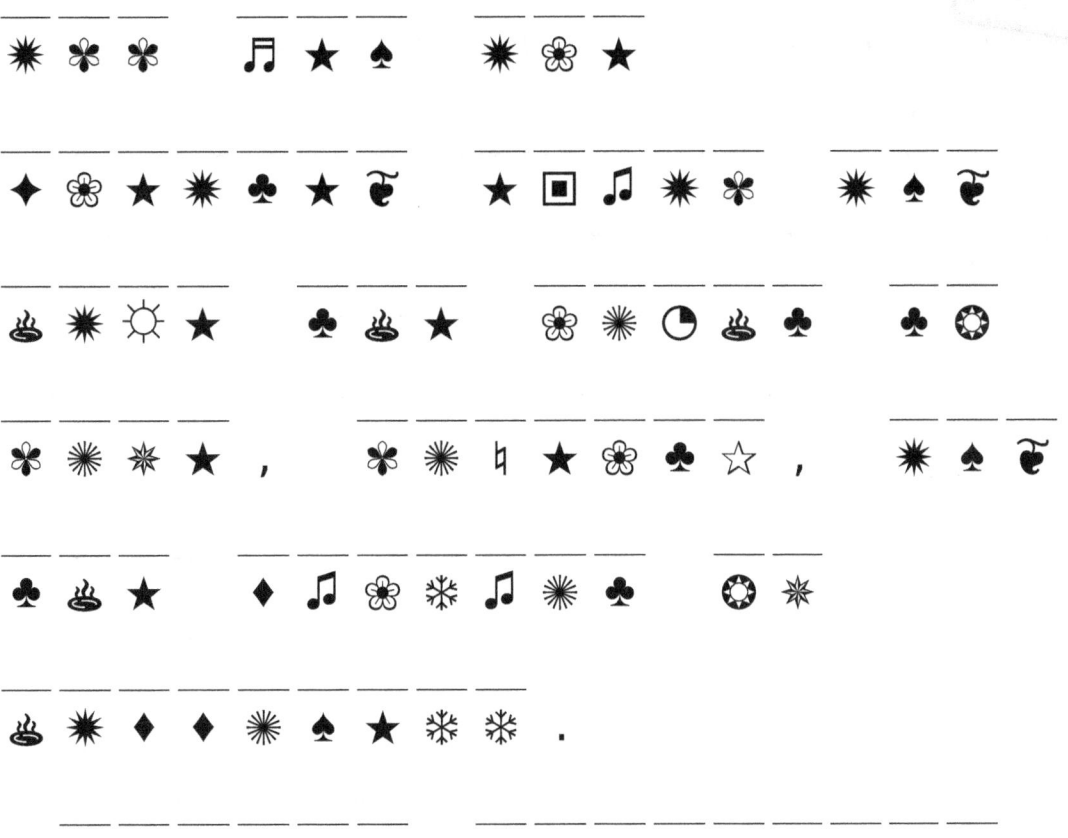

A	B	C	D	E	F	G	H	I	J	K	L	M
✸	♮	◆	☙	★	✻	◔	♨	✺	⁑	✳	❀	♫

N	O	P	Q	R	S	T	U	V	W	X	Y	Z
♠	◎	◆	▣	❀	❄	♣	♪	☼	♥	♌	☆	★

Words Within Words
Veteran

How many words can you make from the word "veteran?"

_____   _____   _____

_____   _____   _____

_____   _____   _____

_____   _____   _____

_____   _____   _____

_____   _____   _____

_____   _____   _____

_____   _____   _____

_____   _____   _____

_____   _____   _____

_____   _____   _____

_____   _____   _____

_____   _____

_____   _____

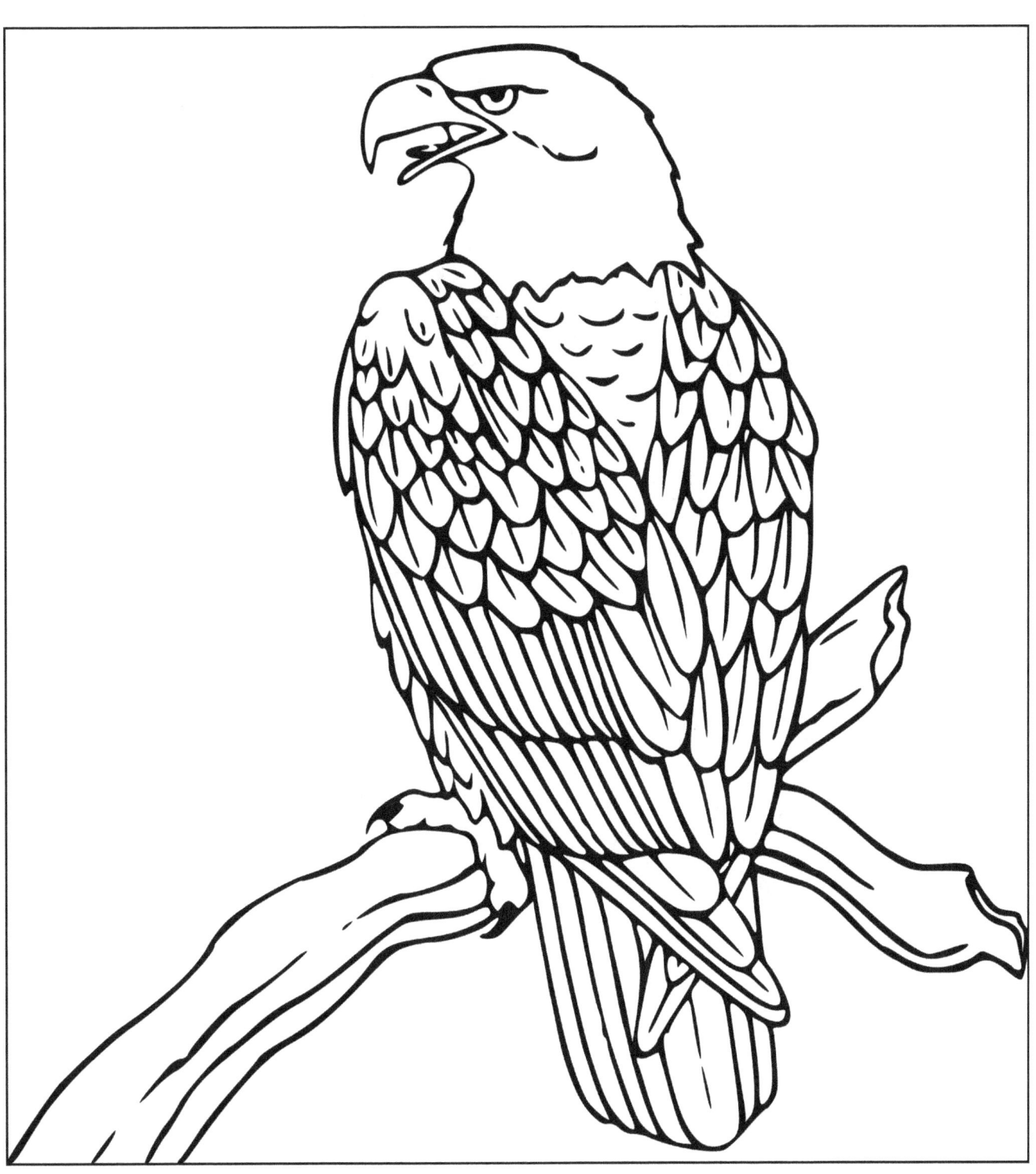

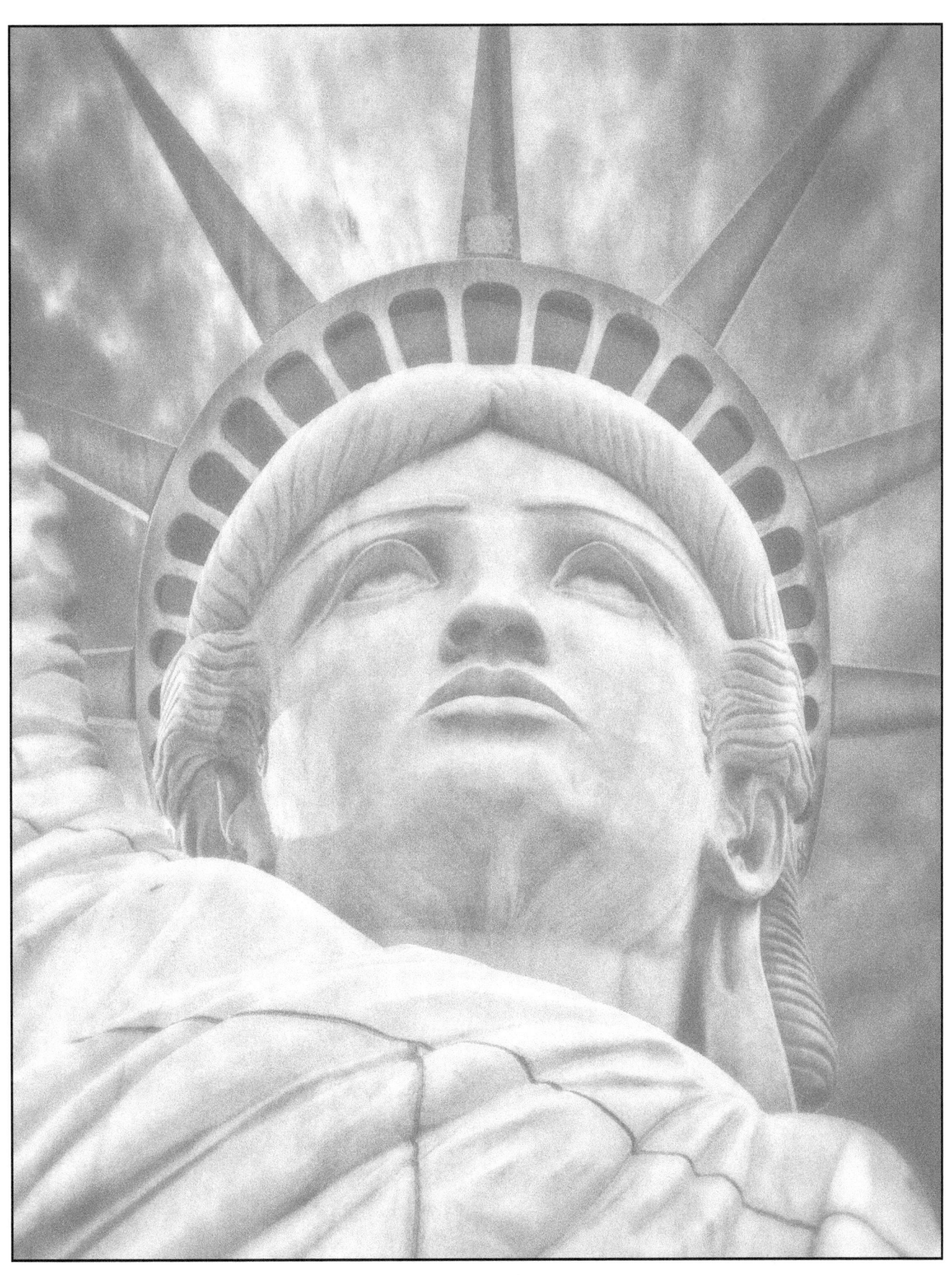

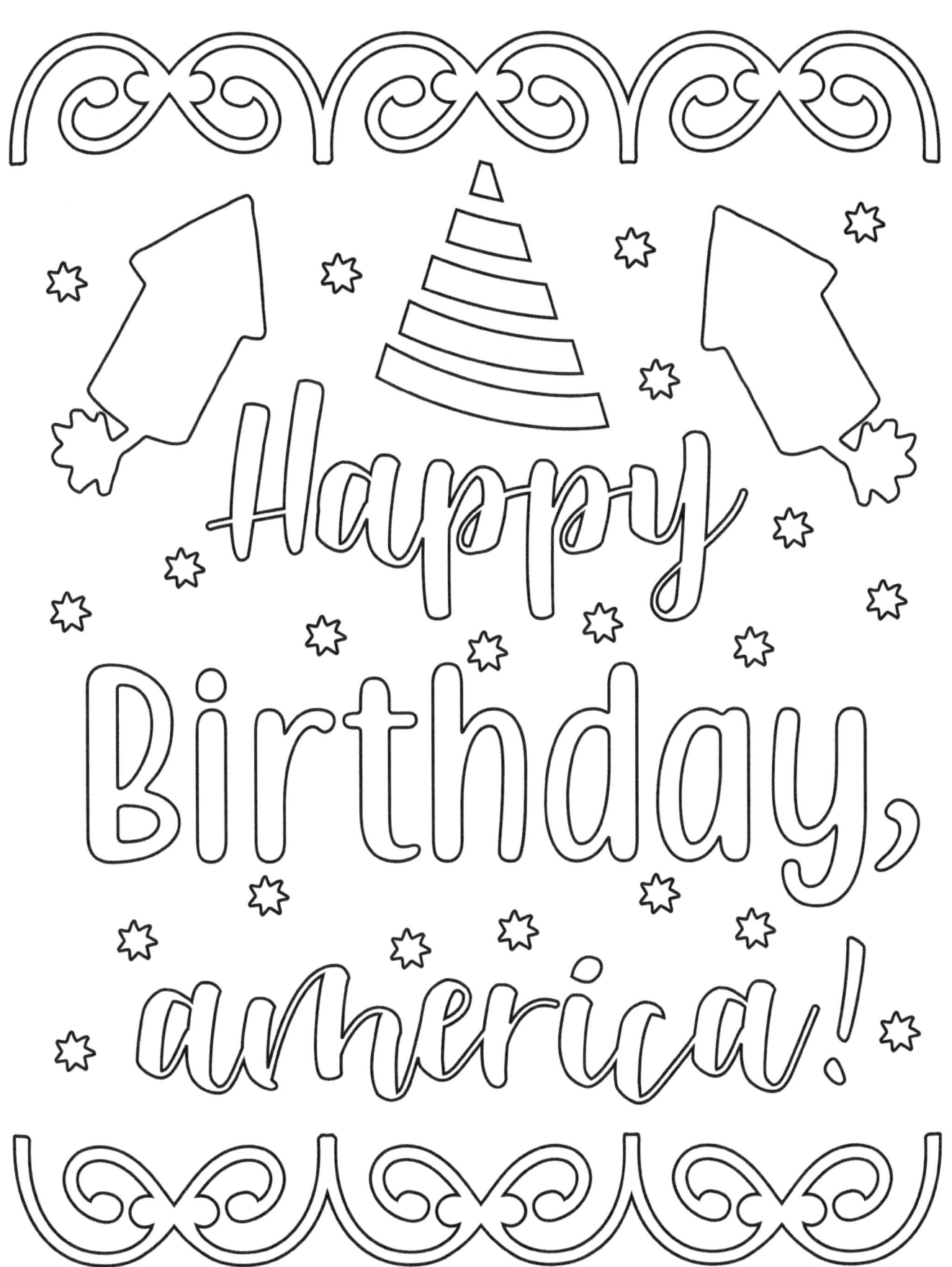

Maze
USA

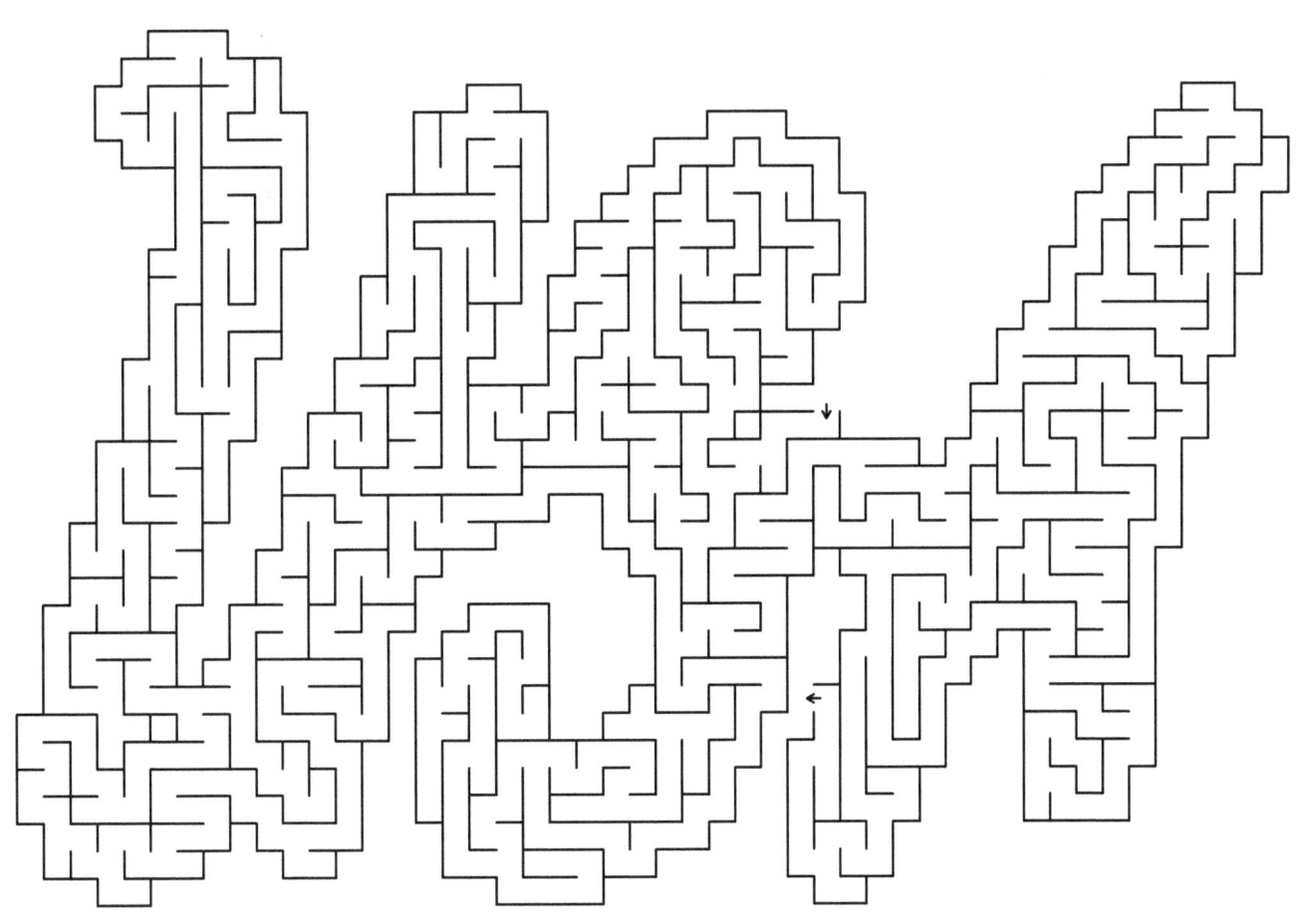

Wordoku
Splendour

	S							P	
			U	S	P	E		
				E				
		D						O
			R	D				
N					O	S	E	
	N			P				E
S			D					
R	U				S		O	N

_____

_____

_____

_____

_____

_____

_____

_____

_____

_____

_____

_____

_____

_____

_____

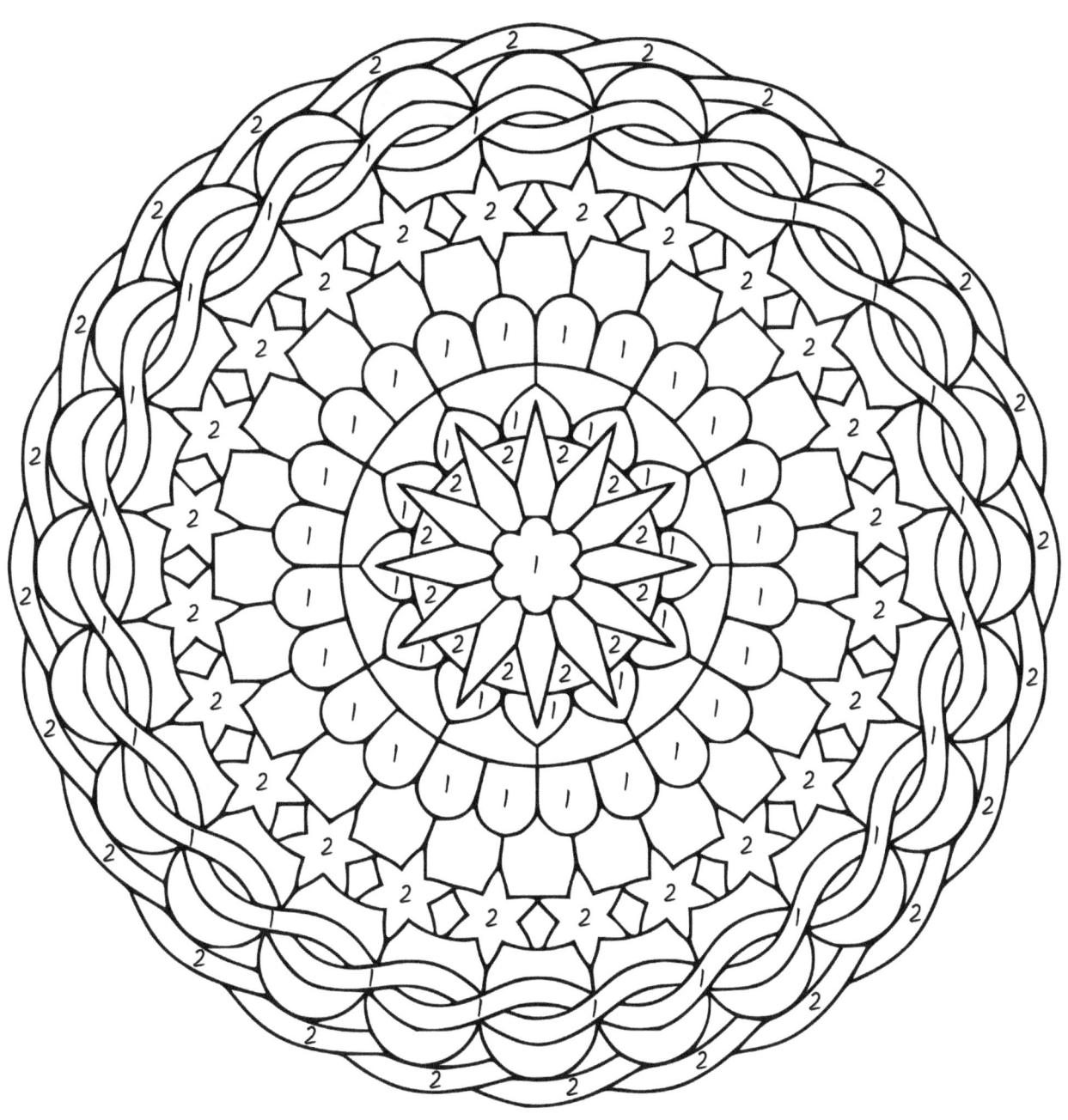

1 = Red
2 = Dark Blue

Maze
Uncle Sam Hat

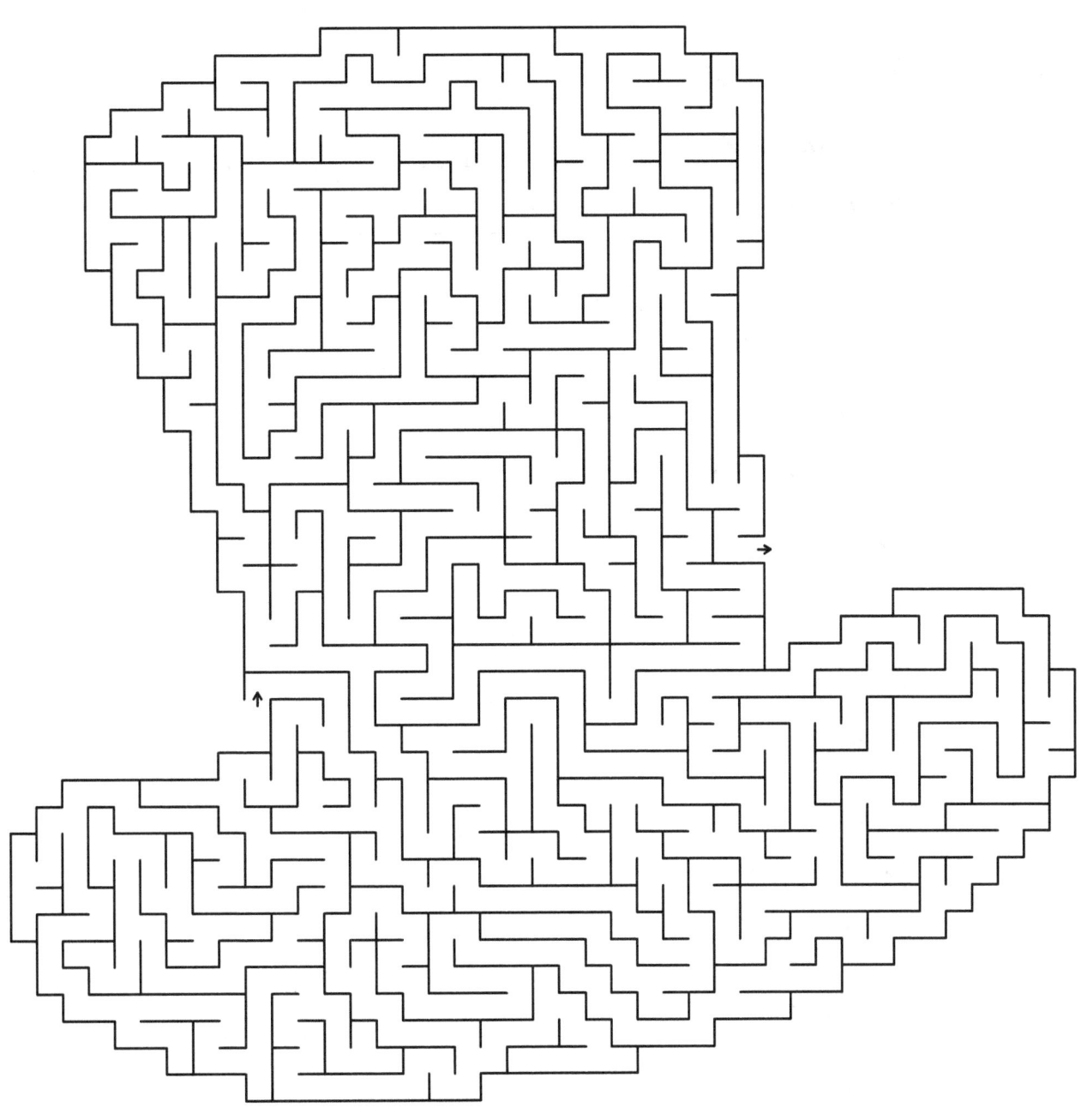

Word Scramble
America's Independence

Unscramble the following words.

hpaeihpdilal _____

wnhiogastn _____

blelbietrly _____

idfabteetll _____

etstpirsadasnsr _____

noblteacier _____

uotstnniicto _____

iuonoevrlt _____

iodlracntae _____

hoeraetsfrf _____

odeefmr _____

yllorogd _____

istfihlbrolg _____

reabloitni _____

esdilrso _____

lloanico _____

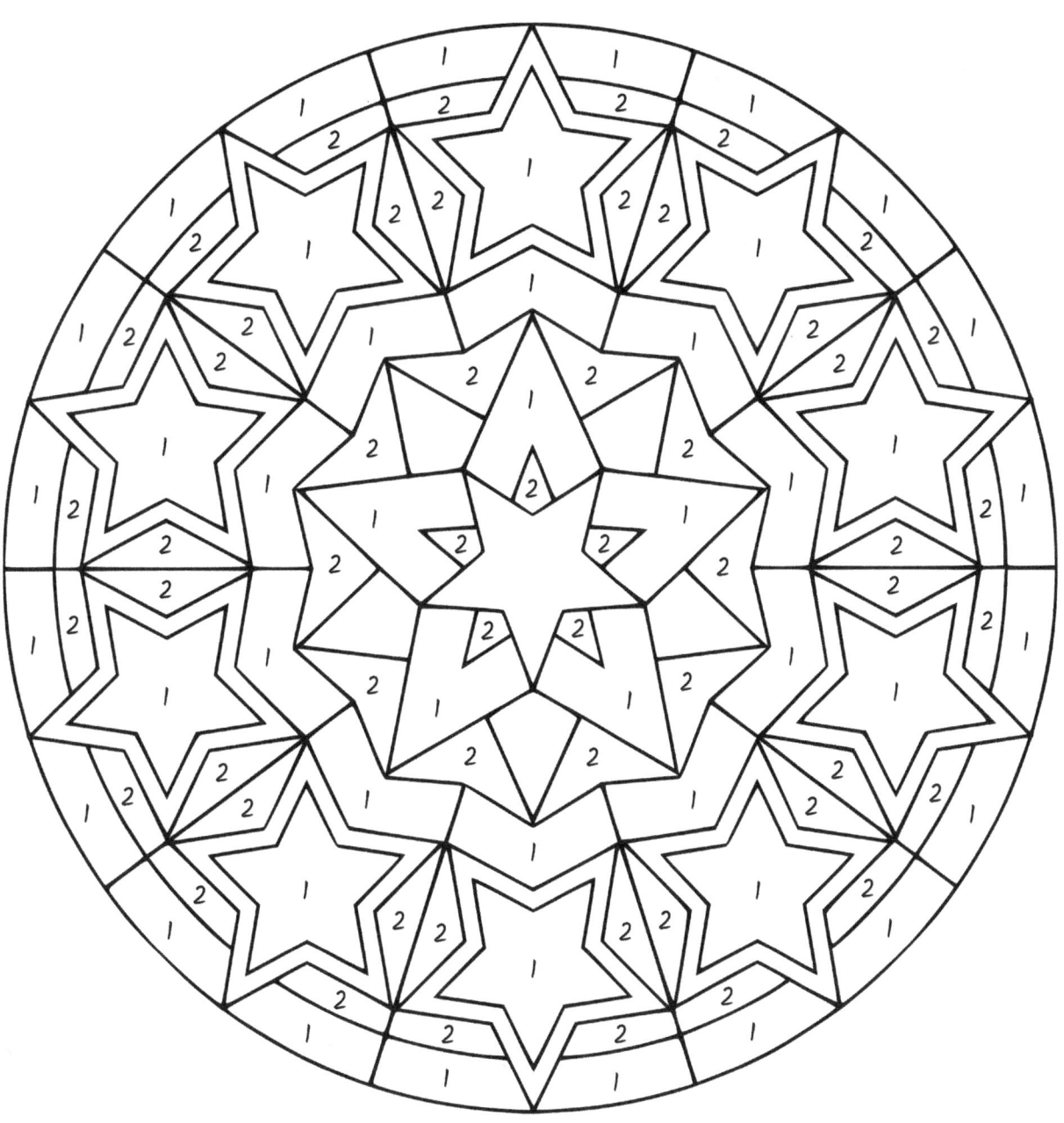

1 = Red
2 = Dark Blue

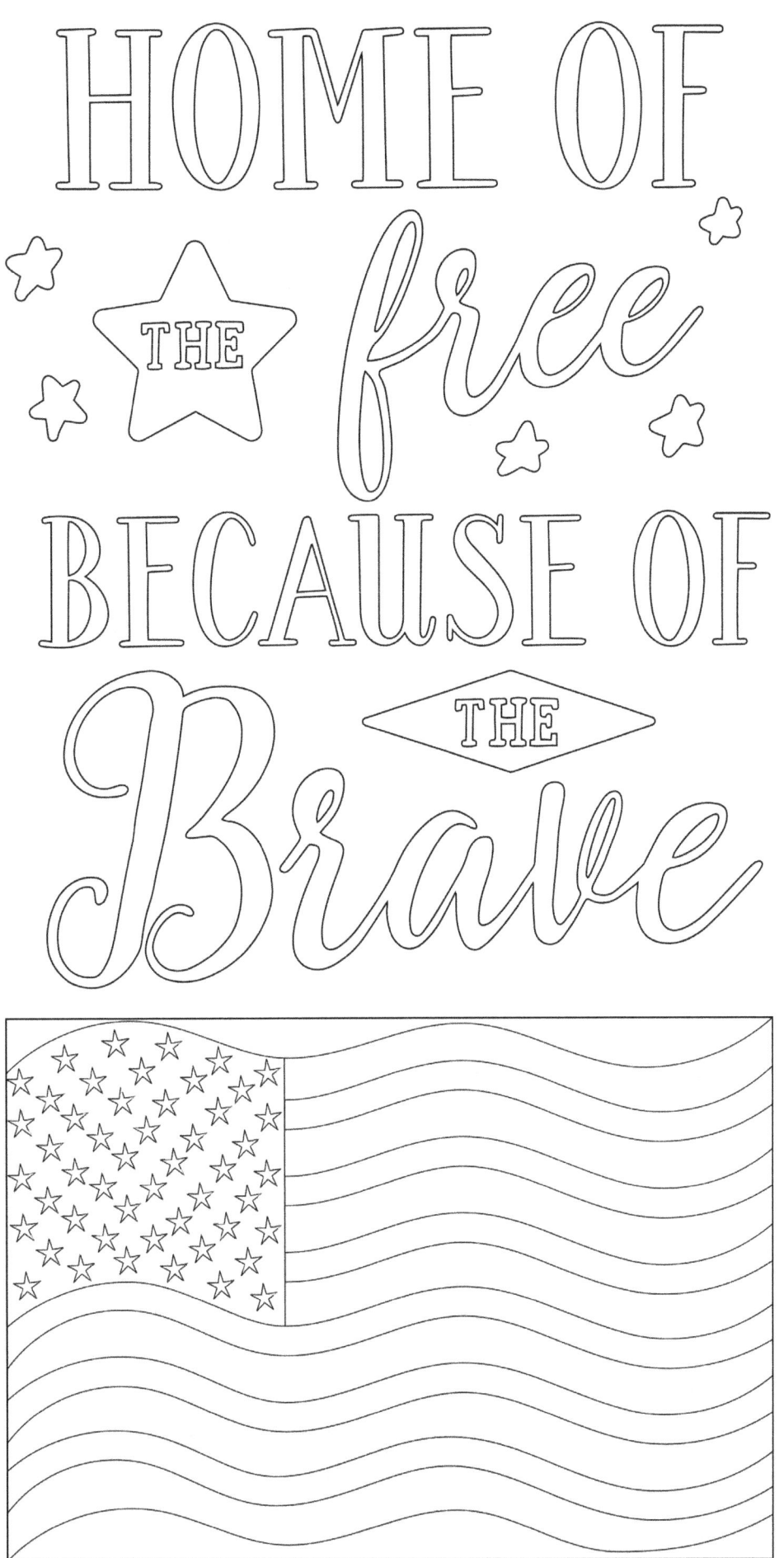

_____

_____

_____

_____

_____

_____

_____

_____

_____

_____

_____

_____

_____

_____

_____

_____

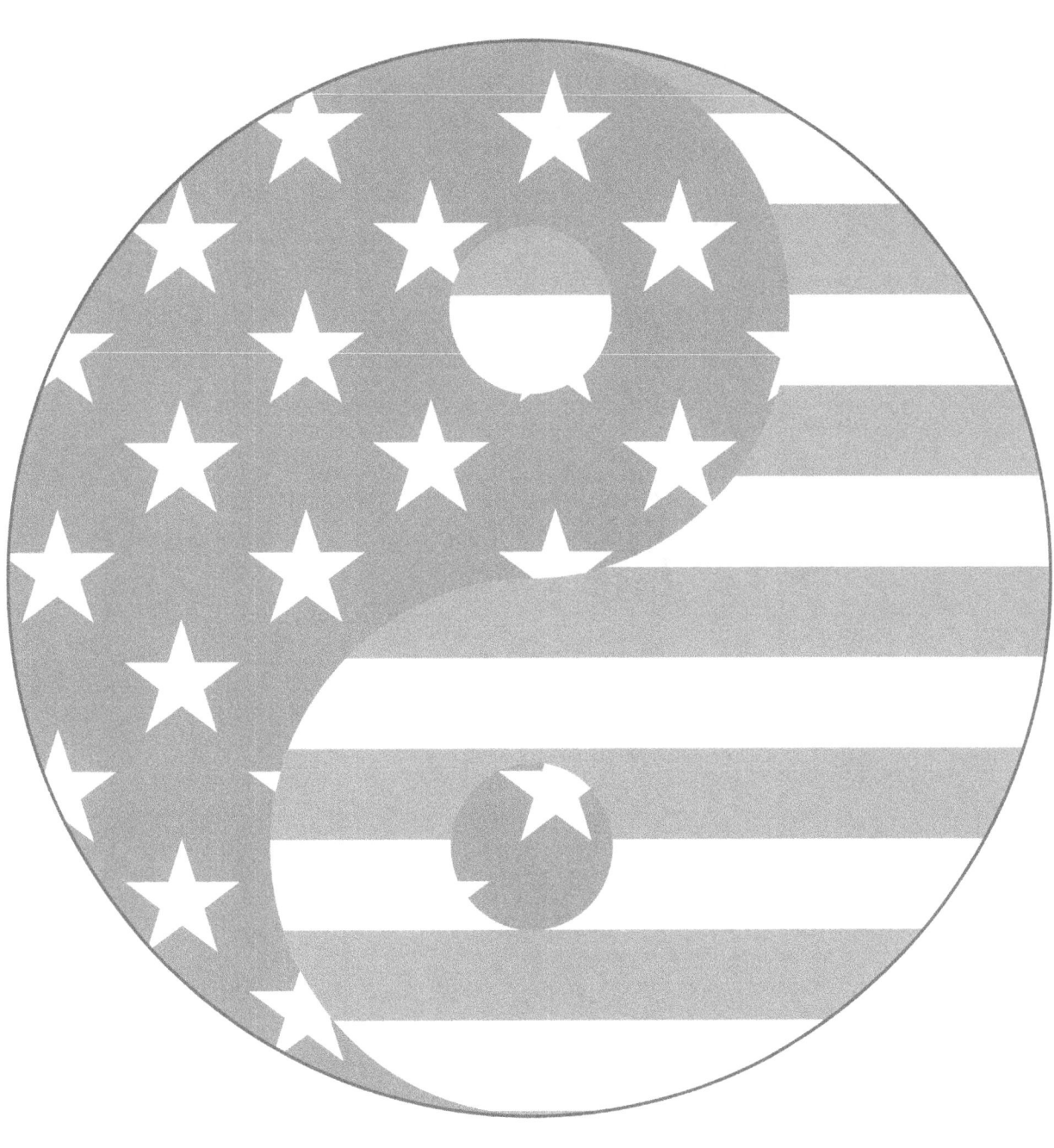

Puzzle
Solutions

Puzzle Solutions
Color By Numbers

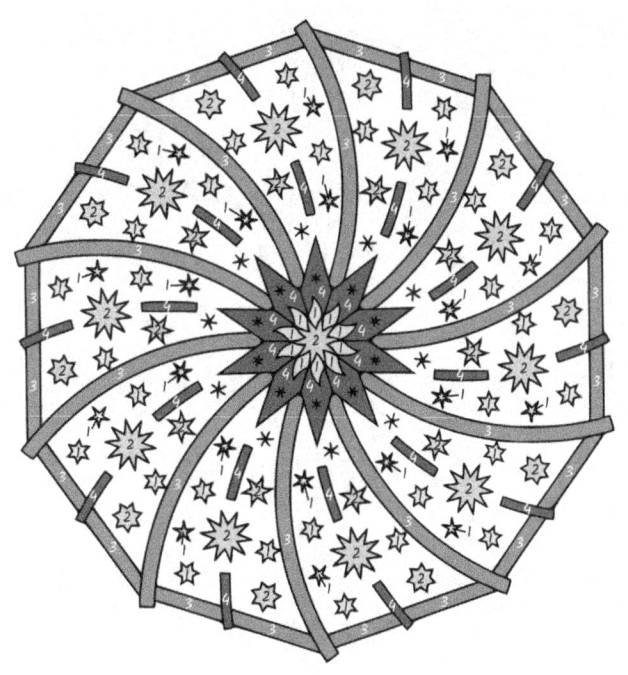

Page 19

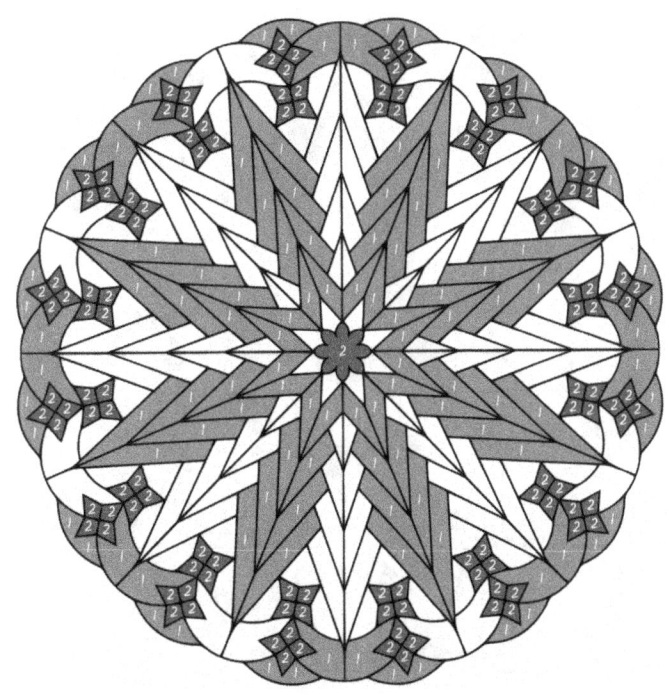

Page 43

Puzzle Solutions
Color By Numbers

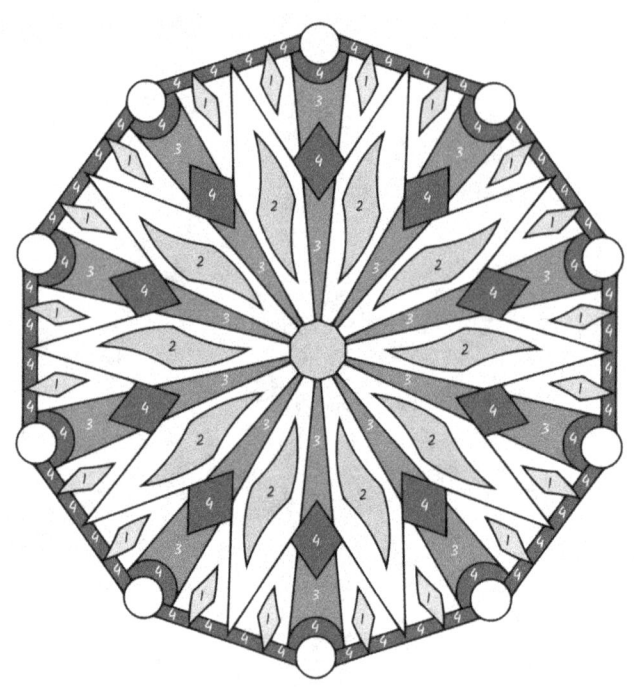

Page 57

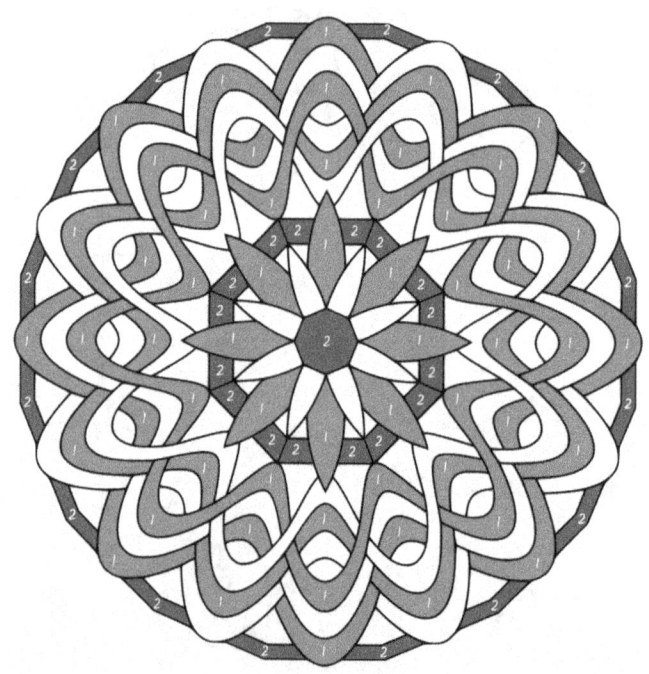

Page 75

Puzzle Solutions
Color By Numbers

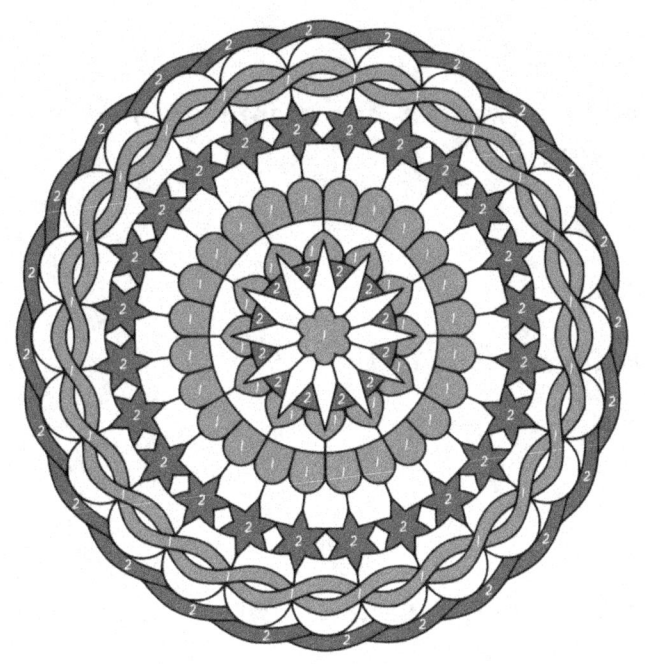

Page 99

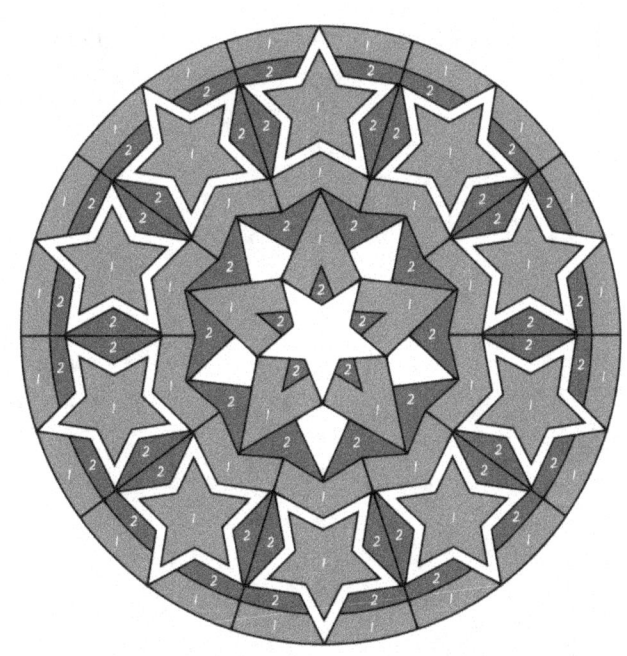

Page 105

Puzzle Solutions
Cryptograms

Page 29
May the sun in his course visit no land more free, more happy, more lovely than this our own country!
-Daniel Webster

Page 53
This nation will remain the land of the free only so long as it is the home of the brave.
-Elmer Davis

Page 69
I know not what course others may take, but as for me, give me liberty or give me death!
-Patrick Henry

Page 85
All men are created equal and have the right to life, liberty, and the pursuit of happiness.
-Thomas Jefferson

Puzzle Solutions
Dot-to-Dot

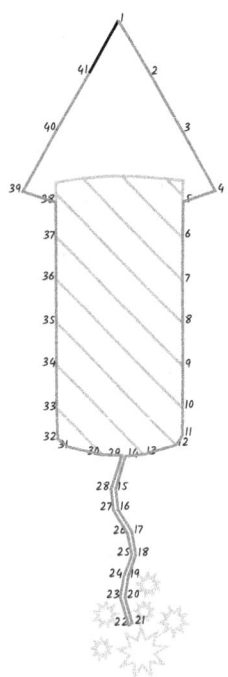

Page 41

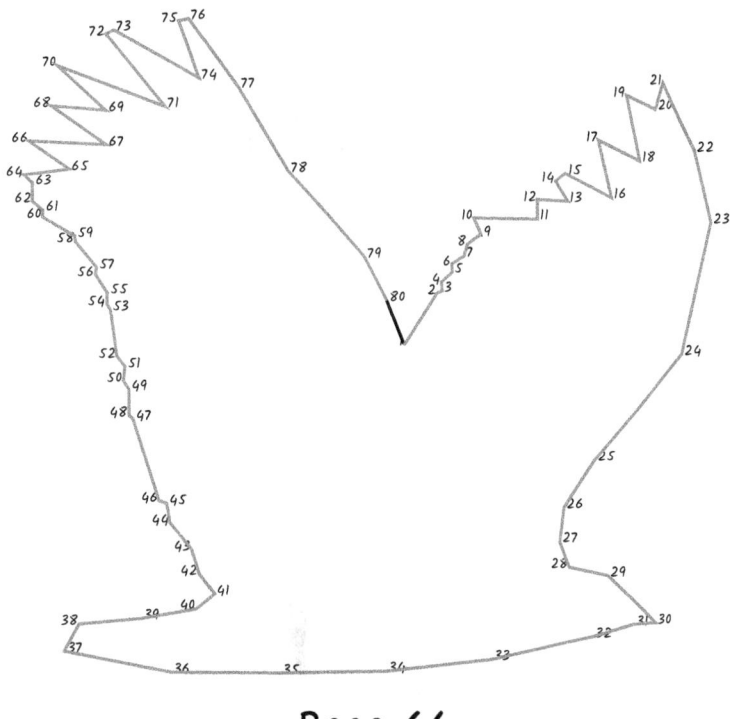

Page 64

Puzzle Solutions
Mazes

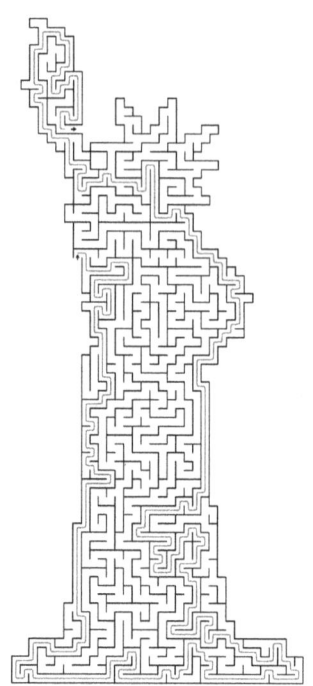

Page 23

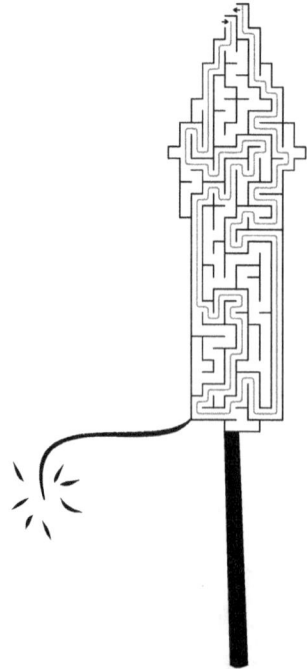

Page 45

Puzzle Solutions
Mazes

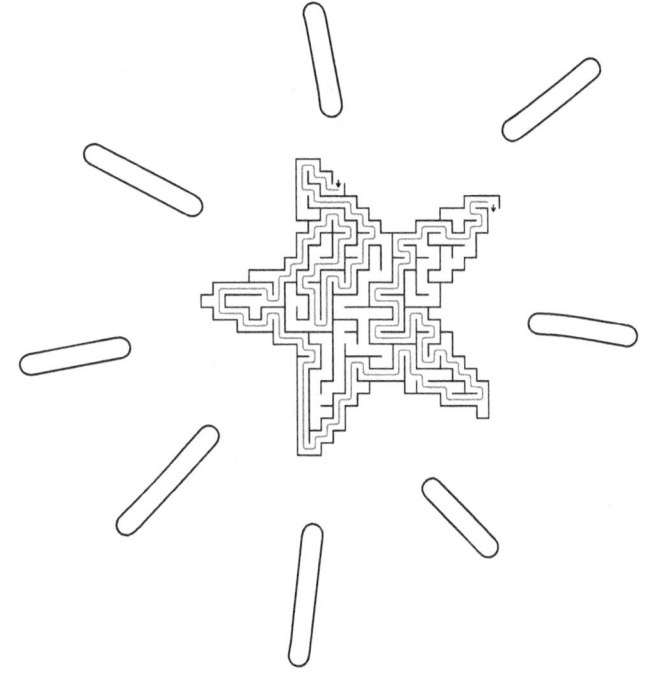

Page 55

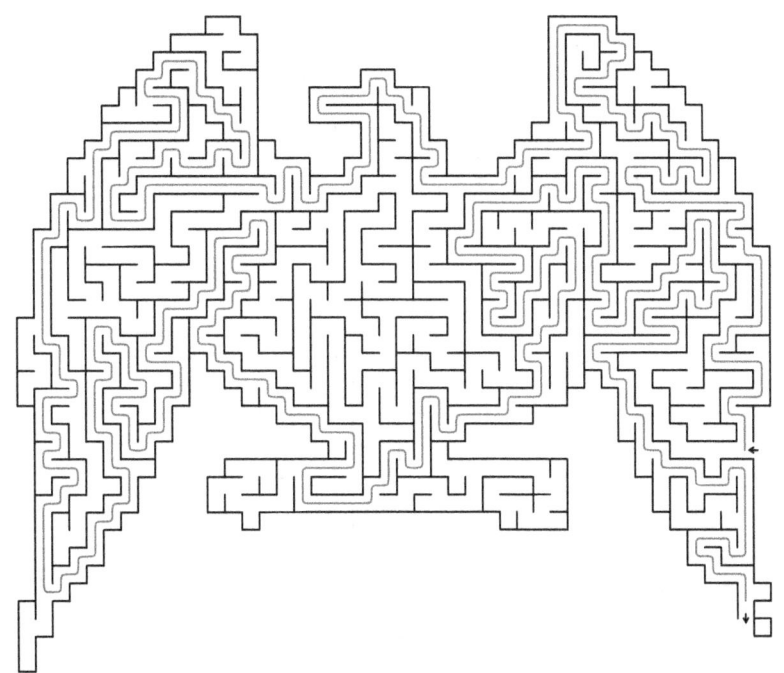

Page 79

Puzzle Solutions
Mazes

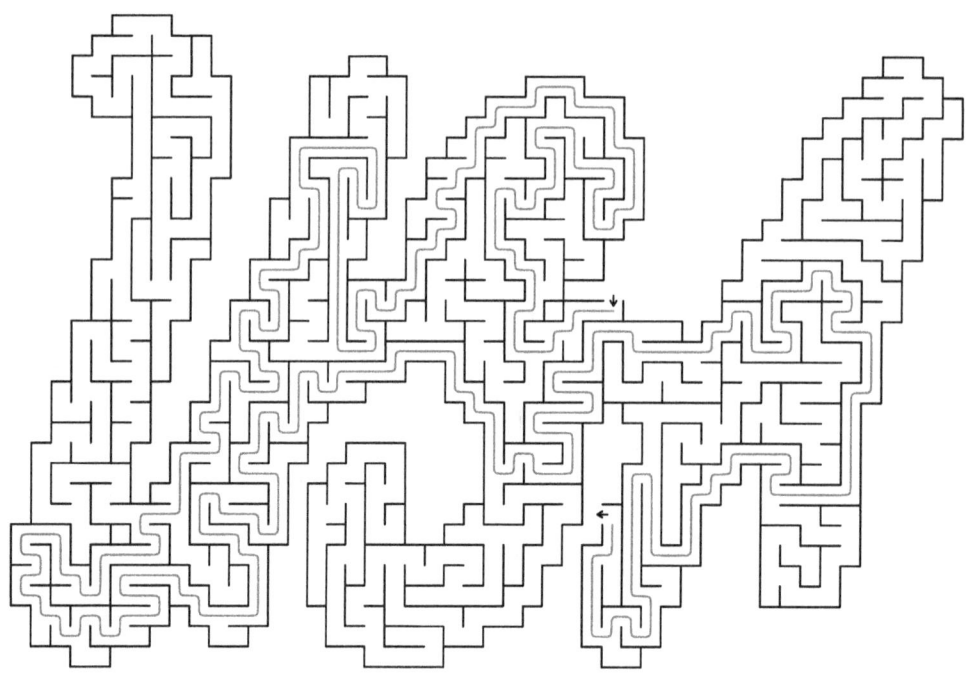

Page 95

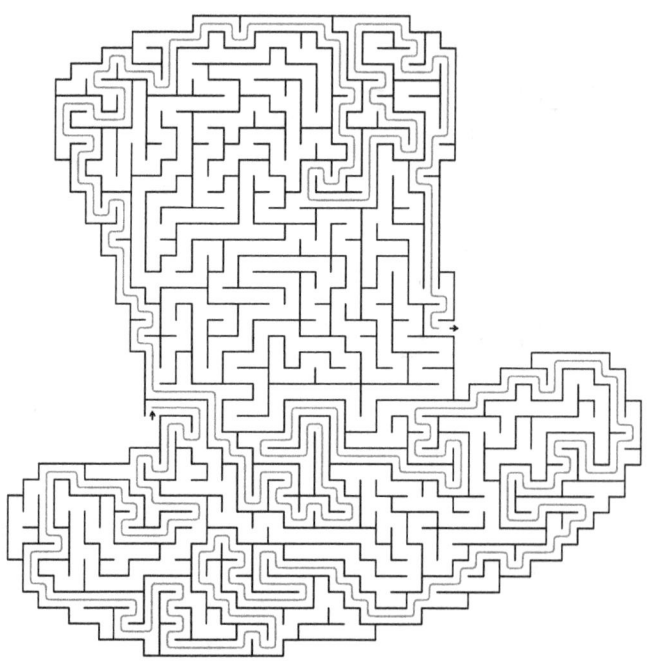

Page 103

Puzzle Solutions
Word Scrambles

Page 54
July 4th Celebration

aburcbee	barbecue
eelpipap	apple pie
omewrtlnea	watermelon
baietoencrl	celebration
amomerteocm	commemorate
naoioedcrt	decoration
fvtilesa	festival
srkceraefcir	firecrackers
ghnariegt	gathering
iegyttlr	glittery
msicu	music
pihenslew	pinwheels
prasrksle	sparklers
oreksct	rockets
erevecren	reverence
remrsatse	streamers

Page 104
America's Independence

hpaeihpdilal	Philadelphia
wnhiogastn	Washington
blelbietrly	Liberty Bell
idfabteetll	battlefield
etstpirsadasnsr	stars and stripes
noblteacier	celebration
uotstnniicto	constitution
iuonoevrlt	revolution
iodlracntae	declaration
hoeraetsfrf	forefathers
odeefmr	freedom
yllorogd	Old Glory
istfihlbrolg	Bill of Rights
reabloitni	liberation
esdilrso	soldiers
lloanico	colonial

Puzzle Solutions
Word Searches

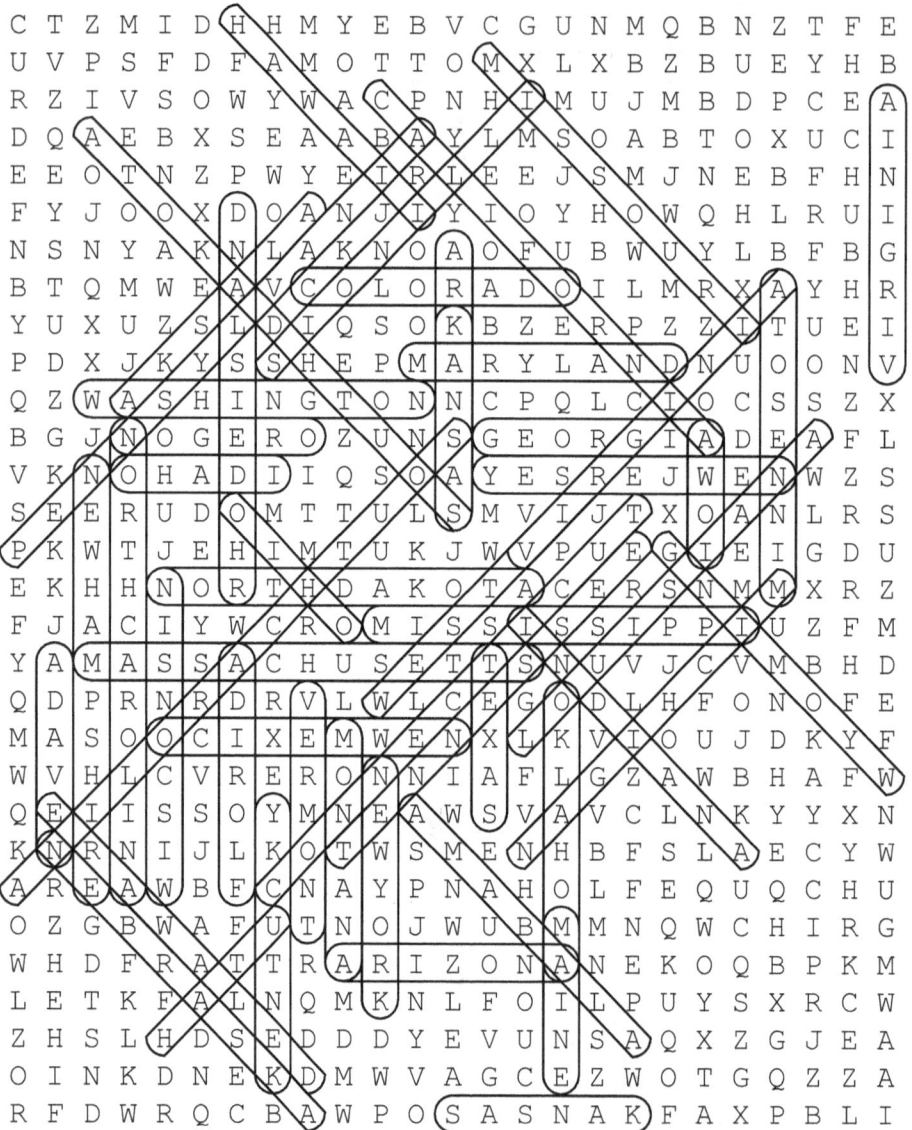

The 50 States, Page 30

Puzzle Solutions
Word Searches

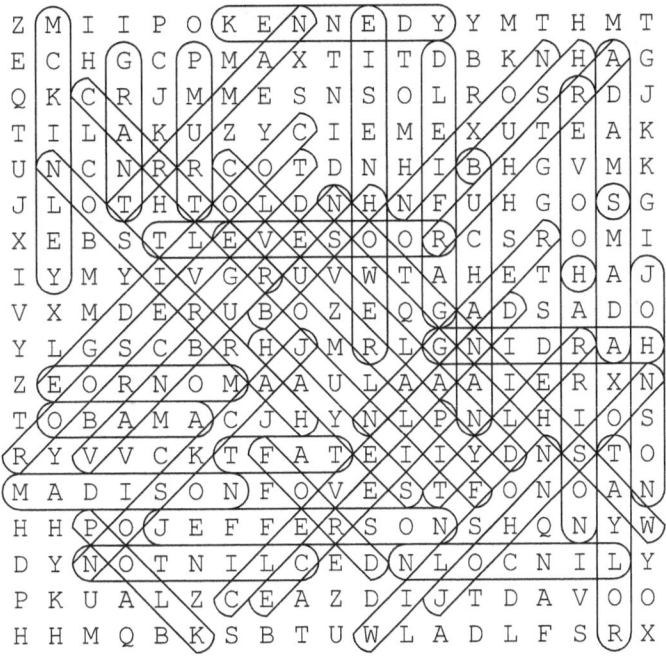

US Presidents, Page 62

Puzzle Solutions
Wordoku

P	L	N	A	K	I	S	R	G
A	K	I	G	R	S	N	L	P
R	G	S	L	N	P	A	K	I
K	I	G	S	L	A	P	N	R
S	P	R	K	I	N	L	G	A
N	A	L	R	P	G	K	I	S
L	S	K	P	G	R	I	A	N
G	N	P	I	A	K	R	S	L
I	R	A	N	S	L	G	P	K

Sparkling, Page 24

E	N	C	G	M	I	L	O	W
W	M	G	L	E	O	I	N	C
I	O	L	C	N	W	M	E	G
L	I	W	N	G	M	O	C	E
G	E	N	I	O	C	W	L	M
O	C	M	E	W	L	N	G	I
N	W	I	O	C	G	E	M	L
M	G	O	W	L	E	C	I	N
C	L	E	M	I	N	G	W	O

Welcoming, Page 42

Puzzle Solutions
Wordoku

O	D	F	U	W	L	E	R	N
R	L	N	D	O	E	W	U	F
W	E	U	R	F	N	D	L	O
L	F	O	N	E	U	R	D	W
U	R	D	W	L	O	F	N	E
E	N	W	F	D	R	L	O	U
N	U	E	L	R	W	O	F	D
F	W	R	O	N	D	U	E	L
D	O	L	E	U	F	N	W	R

Wonderful, Page 56

N	I	S	O	T	E	L	C	A
C	A	T	L	I	S	N	O	E
E	O	L	C	N	A	T	S	I
S	E	I	T	C	L	O	A	N
L	T	O	N	A	I	C	E	S
A	N	C	E	S	O	I	T	L
T	C	A	I	E	N	S	L	O
O	S	N	A	L	T	E	I	C
I	L	E	S	O	C	A	N	T

Coastline, Page 70

Puzzle Solutions
Wordoku

Y	E	V	S	C	R	O	I	D
R	S	O	Y	D	I	V	C	E
D	I	C	V	O	E	S	Y	R
O	Y	R	C	E	S	I	D	V
V	D	E	O	I	Y	C	R	S
S	C	I	D	R	V	Y	E	O
C	R	D	I	S	O	E	V	Y
I	V	S	E	Y	D	R	O	C
E	O	Y	R	V	C	D	S	I

Discovery, Page 80

L	S	E	N	O	D	U	P	R
O	R	N	U	S	P	E	D	L
P	D	U	L	E	R	O	N	S
U	P	D	S	N	E	L	R	O
E	O	S	R	D	L	N	U	P
N	L	R	P	U	O	S	E	D
D	N	L	O	P	U	R	S	E
S	E	O	D	R	N	P	L	U
R	U	P	E	L	S	D	O	N

Splendour, Page 96

Page 32
Bravery

Three Letter Words

are	aye	bay	ear	err	rye
ave	bar	bye	era	ray	yea

Four Letter Words

bare	brae	rare	rear	verb	year
bear	bray	rave	vary	very	

Five Letter Words

barre	berry	brave	rebar	yerba

Six Letter Words

braver	brayer

Page 46
Freedom

Three Letter Words

doe	fed	foe	fro	ore	rod
ere	fee	for	ode	red	roe

Four Letter Words

deem	dorm	fore	from	more	reef
deer	feed	form	mere	redo	rode
dome	ford	free	mode	reed	

Five Letter Words

defer	erode	freed	refed

Six Letter Words

deform	formed

Page 61
Liberty

Three Letter Words

bet	let	lit	rib	tie	tye
bit	lie	lye	rye	try	yet
bye					

Four Letter Words

belt	brie	lire	rely	tier	tire
bile	byte	lyre	rile	tile	yeti
bite					

Five Letter Words

beryl	liter	litre	relit	tiler	tribe
biter					

Six Letter Words

riblet

Page 86
Veteran

Three Letter Words

ant	eat	eve	rat	tea	van
are	era	net	tan	tee	vat
art	ere	ran	tar	ten	vet
ear					

Four Letter Words

ante	even	neat	rave	tear	vane
earn	ever	rant	rent	teen	veer
eave	near	rate	tare	tree	vent

Five Letter Words

avert	eater	event	nerve	never	raven
eaten	enter				

Six Letter Words

neater	tavern

Thank You!!!

Thank you for purchasing this activity book. I hope it brings you hours of fun, enjoyment, and relaxation.

Do you want more? How about free coloring pages, puzzles, and journal pages? Subscribe to the Color Me Peaceful Newsletter, and receive:

♦ A free sample activity book in pdf format (an $8.95 value);

♦ Freebies for subscribers only, including at least one new design* every month;

♦ Fun coloring tips, tricks, and techniques;

♦ Alerts when new designs, pages, and books are released;

♦ Discounts on coloring supplies;

♦ Special offers only for subscribers;

♦ and Much more!!!

*Free designs include coloring pages, puzzles, journal pages, and more.

Visit colormepeaceful.com/newsletter/ to sign up.
(Please Note: TNT Crafts/Color Me Peaceful does not sell or rent subscriber names, customer names, or other private account information to third parties and has no intention of doing so in the future.)

You can see other original activity books, coloring books and pages, puzzle books, and journals from Color Me Peaceful at these websites.

♦ Color Me Peaceful: colormepeaceful.com

♦ Etsy Shop: https://ColorMePeacefulbyTNT.etsy.com

Again, thank you for your purchase. If you have any questions or comments, please e-mail me at: info @ colormepeaceful.com.

About the Author

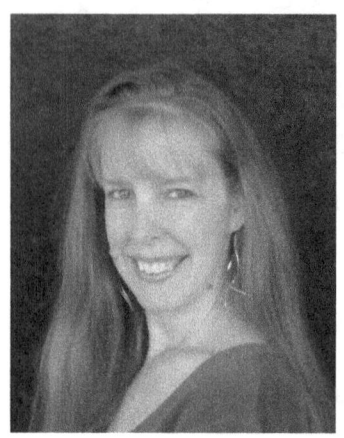

Teresa Nichole Thomas has been passionate about all things crafty--whether physical or digital--since she was a young girl. She has carried this passion into adulthood and has produced many adult coloring pages and books, designed hundreds of beading tutorials, created numerous digital scrapbooking pages, and developed various new Vegan recipes.

When Teresa is not creating, she uses her other passion of healthy eating to show others that healthy food can be delightful and interesting (in a good way) and can taste fabulous. Because of this passion and her own struggles with food, she became a Master Certified Transformational Nutrition Coach. In this role, she helps women who are struggling to lose weight to finally lose it once and for all.

Through her passions, she strives for balance and hopes to inspire and encourage all those she encounters to always find what makes their hearts and souls sing, to be authentic, and to follow their hearts.

You can visit Teresa at:
colormepeaceful.com
tntcrafts.com
harmonyandzen.com